Let Me Count the Ways

A MEMOIR

Tomás Q. Morín

University of Nebraska Press   Lincoln

Portions of the book originally appeared in "Mannish Boy," *Prairie Schooner* 89, no. 4 (Winter 2015); "Table Talk," *Threepenny Review* 153 (Spring 2018); and "Mannish Boy: An Excerpt," *Hinchas de Poesía* 18 (2016).

The University of Nebraska Press is part of a land-grant institution with campuses and programs on the past, present, and future homelands of the Pawnee, Ponca, Otoe-Missouria, Omaha, Dakota, Lakota, Kaw, Cheyenne, and Arapaho Peoples, as well as those of the relocated Ho-Chunk, Sac and Fox, and Iowa Peoples.

Publication of this volume was assisted by the School of Humanities and the Office of Research at Rice University.

Library of Congress
Cataloging-in-Publication Data
Names: Morín, Tomás Q., author.
Title: Let me count the ways: a memoir / Tomás Q. Morín.
Description: Lincoln: University of Nebraska Press, 2022. | Series: American lives
Identifiers: LCCN 2021033066
ISBN 9781496226495 (paperback)
ISBN 9781496231130 (epub)
ISBN 9781496231147 (pdf)
Subjects: LCSH: Morín, Tomás Q.—Mental health. | Obsessive-compulsive disorder—Patients—Biography. | Compulsive behavior. | BISAC: BIOGRAPHY & AUTOBIOGRAPHY / Personal Memoirs
Classification: LCC RC533 .M672 2022 | DDC 616.85/2270092 [B]—dc23/eng/20211001
LC record available at https://lccn.loc.gov/2021033066

Set in Janson Text LT Pro by Mikala R. Kolander.
Designed by L. Auten.

The names and identifying details of some people have been changed. There are no composite characters in this book.

para mi mamá,
Bertha E. Quintana
y
mi abuela,
Victoria E. Quintana

Happy families are all alike; every unhappy family is unhappy in its own way.

—Leo Tolstoy, *Anna Karenina*
   (translated by Constance Garnett)

All happy families resemble one another, each unhappy family is unhappy in its own way.

—Leo Tolstoy, *Anna Karenina*
   (translated by Louise and Aylmer Maude)

All happy families are alike; each unhappy family is unhappy in its own way.

—Leo Tolstoy, *Anna Karenina*
   (translated by Richard Pevear and Larissa Volokhonsky)

Obsessive-Compulsive Disorder (OCD) is a common, chronic and long-lasting disorder in which a person has uncontrollable, reoccurring thoughts (obsessions) and behaviors (compulsions) that he or she feels the urge to repeat over and over.

Obsessions are repeated thoughts, urges, or mental images that cause anxiety. Compulsions are repetitive behaviors that a person with OCD feels the urge to do in response to an obsessive thought.

—National Institute of Mental Health

Contents

LET ME COUNT THE WAYS

On Counting

The green light is long and traffic is thick. My car inches forward.
I count nearly everything I see. Sidewalks, stairs, cars, the tires
and doors of those cars, not to mention the blocks they are parked
alongside. On other days, I've counted little things, too: books,
forks, carpets, shadows, chairs, even people's feet. Once, I even
counted the soft-blue stripes of a man's shirt. I can't tell you what
year it was or if I saw him in Chicago, Provincetown, Santa Cruz,
or somewhere else. I can't even remember whom I was with or
even what I was wearing. But the stripes, the thumbnail-thick
ocean-blue stripes on white cotton, were like the bars of a fence
behind which was a land of peace I had only dreamed of. In all
the years my memory has carried the stripes from some random
person's shirt, they have never changed.

My counting is not most people's counting. I never drove
through a city like some human adding machine, the city limits
sign in my rearview and my head buzzing with numbers. What
good would it be to anyone if I knew that on a certain day in
a certain year, I saw twenty-six spoons moving in and out of
twenty-six bowls in a restaurant you've never been to? There

was no 1, 2, 3 for me. I have no desire to tangle with a string of numbers you can wind around the planet until the end of time.

Two more cars. Two more cars and I can turn left.

I blink my left eye when I line up with the ass end of a car, then blink my right eye when I'm at the center, and the left again when I reach the front bumper.

I've done this for every car on the street since I left my apartment. The slow traffic has made this block easier, a block whose start, middle, and end I also mark. And every building on this block and the windows and doors of each building. At least as many of them as I can. These patterns are something I can depend on. They are inviolable, perfect, and all my own.

The traffic is finally moving, and the palm trees I love are in the rearview. Sometimes when a certain itch creeps into my spirit and I feel misplaced, I'll scratch it by making the block and driving slow, because the palms against the wall of the white stucco Methodist church can trick you into thinking you could be on a side street of an island, instead of in the middle of Texas. My mother's grandfather used to say his family was from the Canary Islands. People say time moves slower on an island. That would be nice if it were true, but I don't believe it. Time is time, isn't it?

Going downhill now.

Ten minutes and I'll be home.

Since my eyes can't keep up with all the counting now that I'm driving faster, I also tap my fingers and toes, clench and unclench my jaw, even flex the muscles of my arms and legs when the blocks are particularly crowded. While I'm driving and thinking about not breaking any traffic laws and where I am going and the time of day and thus how long before the sun goes down and countless other things, I also have in my head LeftRightLeftRightLeftRightLeftRightLeftRightLeftRightLeftRightLeftRight going a mile a minute. For years, I assumed Left Right Left was in everyone else's head too. If you could measure the world and know where everything began and ended, why wouldn't you?

Another left turn and the river is to my right now, and the buildings are fewer and farther apart. I glance at the door locks again. I'm driving over twenty miles an hour. I remind myself there are limits to what a human being can do.

My parents taught me early that their love had its limits. I wish I could have mapped out their love. My counting is a way for me to return the things people have made to the blueprint stage. Since people don't have blueprints, maybe when I count a part of them, like what they're wearing, it's closer to mapping.

I wish I could have set their love for one another like islands against a field of oceans and wrapped them tight with an equator.

Park. Ignition off. Windows up. Parking brake. Keys and phone in my right hand, wallet in the left. I stay off the grass, because some people don't pick up after their dogs. Inside, I put my things away, and the Virgen de Guadalupe on my dresser reminds me I was given a Bible I haven't read because I don't want to open it and discover one of my favorite parts is missing, the chapter where they begin talking about how so and so begat three sons and two daughters and lived three-hundred-and-forty-something years. Most people probably skip those genealogies (surely most nine-year-olds), but I read every single one of them when I was a kid.

What you miss if you skip the biblical genealogies is how in all that begetting and centuries of death, there was one single break to speak of. The story was written,

And Enoch walked with God after he begat Methuselah
three hundred years, and begat sons and daughters:
And all the days of Enoch were three hundred sixty and
five years:

And Enoch walked with God: and he was not; for God took him.

And that was it, the one break in the divine sequence up to that point. Enoch "was not," meaning he didn't die and was just no more, carried off to someplace else, delivered from all the endless birth and dying. Even though I talked to God all the time when I was a kid, I didn't know what it meant to walk with him. What I did know was how to take the measure of the world, to love the end that everything had coming, even as my own seemed like it would be denied to me forever and ever.

In Our Own Way

I can't remember how old I was the first time I saw my father cook. Four or five, maybe? He was in the front seat of the car, and I was supposed to have my eyes closed in the back. I had never seen him do this at home, though I had wanted to every time I wandered into the kitchen and was quickly shuffled out.

I was impressed the first time I watched him cooking. Who knew a spoon and a bit of cotton was all anyone needed to make some magic happen? He once took a bottle cap and stuck a match on the side of it like a handle. In no time flat he cooked up a bit of heroin in his tiny pot. If there had been a dark version of the Boy Scouts, one focused on hustling and crime, my father would've earned all the badges, been the founder and president, had his handsome face on all the posters and brochures. He could cook faster than it probably takes most people to shampoo. In grade school when someone bragged about their father, I wanted to say, "Oh yeah? Well, my dad can shoot heroin faster than yours!" Or even better, the one that could've won any father bragging contest: "My dad can shoot more heroin than yours and not die!"

Once the heroin was cooked and the cotton had done its work, there was nothing left but to draw it up. He held the needle to the light and flicked it with his hard fingers. The liquid inside was the color of that last pool of iced tea in the bottom of our pitcher I loved to tip and gulp.

My father had the body of an ox. How else could someone shoot heroin for twenty-one years and survive? His body was his blessing and our curse. It kept him alive long enough to kick after he was released from the penitentiary, but it never let him truly hit rock bottom on the outside. Before he could finally kick, doctors discovered that his gallbladder was shot. For so many years, the pain of his withdrawals was his gallbladder screaming for someone to free it from the prison of his body.

For some reason, he never seemed to care about hiding his track marks. Some folks shoot in their legs and all kinds of odd places in order to hide their addiction. Some, even between their toes. No, his favorite spot was the classic one just below the biceps. The same cephalic vein doctors use when they draw blood. He stuck that vein so much over the years, it came to look like a marble was hidden under his skin. It was black, hard, and anyone who saw it knew what it meant.

To this day, I tell nurses to draw from my left arm, because the vein is less pronounced there. If I don't and they use the right, then by the time I get home, the spot they used has risen and rounded off, not unlike the first time I took a pencil and tapped its yellow body with my fingernail before shoving it under the skin of my little arm. I can't remember if I chose my left or right arm, the right or the left.

What I do recall is that the knowledge that I was now a grown-up filled my chest that night. I was no longer a little boy who couldn't be left alone at home. I was a man who owned his body, who could make it bleed when he wanted to. So what, I thought, if I hadn't made my own fire in the back seat? The fire would come in time. Filled with pride, I tapped my mother on the shoulder and showed her the little man I now was.

I-37 BETWEEN MATHIS and Corpus Christi is flat. Even flatter cotton fields, with seemingly no end, surround it.

When people ask where I'm from, a small town near Corpus Christi is what I usually say. When they ask what it's called, I finally relent and say Mathis. I then add how tiny it is (my senior class was about seventy-two strong) and that most people have probably never heard of it. The rare few who have heard of it know it as the place they stop to get gas on their way to South Padre Island or their family's house on Lake Corpus Christi.

Fifteen miles down the road is Edroy. In Mathis, when the gulf breeze blows the smell of cow shit into town, we all think, *Eeed-roy*. After Edroy is Calallen, home to a perennial football powerhouse, the closest movie theater, and one of the hospitals we'd take my father to when he had withdrawals. Farther up the road is Tuloso-Midway, a place some call a suburb of Corpus, though it's no more attached to Corpus than the severed arm of a starfish is to the body to which it once belonged. Pass Tuloso and the road gives way to the refineries whose fires never stop burning as you enter the city, neighborhoods, and houses behind whose doors my father would disappear and find what his mind had no doubt been turning over and over all day as he waited for my mom to get off work.

On payday, as soon as my mom dismissed her students at school and made sure they had all been picked up by their parents, she collected me from my elementary class. My father drove us fast to the bank before it closed to cash her paycheck so that we could start our family tradition of driving to Corpus.

We didn't talk much on these drives. In the back seat of our Oldsmobile Cutlass during one of these trips, for the first time, I blinked in a way that evolution hadn't intended.

Left eye.
Right eye.
Left eye.

My father would've been thirty-four on that day, almost ten years younger than I am now. His hair hadn't peppered yet. It was still black and caught the light like water at the bottom of a well. He was five feet ten and burnt dark from the long days spent in the sun building expensive houses out of brick or stone or both. Contractors loved him because he worked fast. He could outbid almost any other bricklayer because he worked alone or with a small crew. He could keep more of the money this way.

I loved walking through the houses he was building. Without carpet, furniture, or paint, they were soft and empty like his eyes. At least once during these trips to Corpus, he would catch me in the rearview mirror staring at him. His face was all sharp angles: nose, cheekbones, and an arrow for a chin whose sharpness was exaggerated by his thin sideburns that dropped down from a mass of wavy hair. His eyebrows were like crow wings at sunset. Straddling his full purple lips was a mustache shaped like a frown.

Next to my father is my mother. She is a few inches shorter than he is. Her face is soft and has a glow about it. I won't understand how tall she is until I pass her height and realize how much of my life I spent looking up at her small mouth, a mouth she is loathe to bend into a smile in photographs. Black hair, long and parted down the middle, from the back seat I watched the wind blow it toward me for so many years when I was a child. Sometimes it was just hair whipped by the wind, and other times it was like a hand reaching out to me from somewhere devoid of light, a place out of time, where darkness folded in on itself, and where no one ever yearned for rest because nothing ever began or ended.

Bored, I stared at the pools of water ahead of us on the road until they disappeared. I wished one of them would grow until it covered the road so we would have to go home. Deep down, I knew that my father would have found us a way across if my wish had come true. He was nothing if not resourceful. I wanted to be like that, to make what I most desired happen, no matter what.

Left eye.

Right eye.

Left.

When his mind was set, he was like one of the bricks he built houses with. We were the cool cement it nestled and squished around itself.

When I wasn't lost in my daydreams of raging south Texas floods springing from the cracks in 1-37, I counted telephone poles. I blinked the miles away one pole at a time.

Left

Right

Left

Before long, I did this on every trip. Left Right Left until I fell asleep to the hot wind roaring in through the windows. The song our tires had been singing slowed as we climbed the freeways of Corpus. I would wake as we burrowed deep into a neighborhood in search of heroin.

MY FATHER IS HUNTING. While he's busy, my mom takes care of the money and is on lookout. My job is to spot unmarked police cars like my father taught me. If I see one, I'm to call out, "Chota!" Blackwall tires, too many antennas, and extra-dark tint were the telltale signs. As much as I would rather have been home, I gave myself to the excitement of looking for "the enemy."

In a parking lot, he cooks the heroin, ties off his arm, and shoots up. I do as I'm told and don't stare at what I've seen before. Instead, I study the tires of every car, the impenetrability of tint, and count antennas on my fingers over and over. I can count now, and counting is useful. Soon I'll know the shapes of the cars the police use, even if I won't know for a long time what a Ford or

Chevy is. My job is important. I've thought through what might happen if I don't pay attention.

My father could go to jail.

I could be taken away from my mother.

She could lose her job.

And everyone would know our secret.

My father done, I can look now. He floats like pieces of snow on a school day. Sometimes I stare at his smile long enough that I forget the miserable ride in the car. Playing at home is where I want to be, except for when his eyes dance like this.

His brain drowns in liquid joy far away from my mom, the woman who loves him too much, and the shy son he doesn't understand. Just like that and Poof! we are invisible. Gone, too, is the wife and mother of his three older children he abandoned. Poof! and Poof!

Our stomachs full of McDonald's, or KFC, our magic man pulls us back onto the road under the night sky toward the towers of flame on the outskirts of Corpus. It is so dark I can barely make out my parents' faces anymore. Tuloso, Calallen, and Edroy are next. Afterward, the comforting lights of Mathis will finally appear in the distance as orange blobs. They look like lidless eyes in the dark that never blink. They watch everything and see nothing.

MY FATHER'S LOVE life was made for television. Cast Eric Estrada in the lead role, pop the popcorn, and settle in for the movie of the week featuring love, betrayal, and lots of kids. Eight kids to be exact. Since the eighth showed up pretty late on the scene out of nowhere, there could be others out there we don't know about. It was easy for so many years to think of him as a generic adulterer. He played the role of the Latin lover as if it had been written for him. Thinking of him as some Don Juan who couldn't keep his pants zipped made it easier to hate him.

What would increase the drama of our movie would be that except for number eight, the other kids were split between two families living in the same town. In our story, we all know about each other, because Mathis is small. Before he meets my mother, he is a married father of two sons and one daughter. I've always wondered how sudden the break was for them. Was he just gone one day to go live with my mother on North Beach in Corpus Christi, or did he take his time collecting his things, slow to leave the family that adored him? Were those early years his favorite because they were romantic and adventurous, he and my mother every night eating the fish he caught for dinner? My birth meant they would soon return to Mathis and to the judging eyes of a community that wanted to know everything about everyone.

I wonder if he ever mentioned his two families to the many drug counselors he spoke with over the years. Or if the subject ever came up when he was in prison talking to therapists. Surely the inmates he asked to write his letters for him (he was ashamed of his handwriting) knew that the envelopes were going to kids at different addresses. If they did, maybe they assumed the break from one family to the next had been clean.

One thing I had stopped counting was how many years kept passing since I had last seen him. A few years ago, my little brother showed me a photo taken at my father's recent birthday party. This is the photo I show after I've told someone about him. I always say the same things as they study the image.

"I can tell he hasn't used drugs in a long time because of his round belly."

"People say we have the same face."

"He's always been dark. My color is halfway between his and my mom's. Unless I've been out in the sun for too long."

Her family, friends, doctors, counselors, I'm certain everyone told my mother to leave him. She was afraid he wouldn't have anywhere to go, and if he didn't have her salary as a public school teacher to count on, then how would he find what he needed when his money ran out, as it always did, and he became sicker and sicker? She believed that his parents and sisters would blame her if he died. Not even after he took her to Mexico, where he married her as a sign of his commitment (he was still married to his first wife), and destroyed the marriage certificate when they returned to Texas did she leave him. That day was still waiting far into the future.

He was always taking our money for drugs, promising to have it back by Sunday night so I could pay for my lunch at school. And when he didn't make it back in time, he stayed gone until he crawled back later in the week after my mom had swallowed her pride and begged the lunch lady (at the school where my mother was a teacher, no less) to let me eat for a few days without paying.

Where had he been the whole time he was gone? Were the times when my family was scrambling for money the happy days enjoyed by my half brothers and half sisters when their daddy finally came home? I wonder if their faces lit up in the morning when they found him sitting in the kitchen reading the newspaper and drinking a cup of coffee.

Maybe your sorrow has to be balanced by someone else's joy?

My mother might have been the person with the teaching certificate, but my father was also handing out new lessons nearly every week. I would just as soon have not eaten the food the cafeteria was serving—the peas and carrots were dry, and the meatloaf was like something soggy you scraped off your shoe.

My father taught us about pity—the lunch lady's, my teacher's if she discovered my situation, even my ability to pity myself. What if the lunch lady said no? Where did the kids go who couldn't pay? Would they make us sit in an out-of-the-way classroom and stare at each other? A nap would have been better. In my dreams, I ate like a king.

Monday morning, my first-grade class lined up along the wall made of green squares of unglazed tile. Had my mother spoken to the lunch lady already, or to one of the other teachers in the elementary school?

I looked down the hall in both directions but didn't see my mother.

I forgot about my mother and lunch for a second as I ran the tip of my finger along the grooves of white grout.

As I looked down at my feet, I traced the square over and over as the slow minutes passed, until the tiles shook off the school and blobbed into the warm waters of the Gulf of Mexico they resembled, waters whose waves wore tiny whitecaps as they made their way to my feet and crumpled.

Repetition was becoming my magic against what I couldn't control. But such magic wasn't easy. I had to touch the grout with the skin of my finger just right. If I didn't, I had to start the spell over.

"Alright class, let's go. Stay in line."

Kid by kid approached the folding table of the lunch lady where she sat with nothing but a list of names, a money box, and a pen. She may as well have been a judge in a courtroom to me. The protocol was you either showed her a plastic card or gave her money. When it was my turn, I gave her the only thing of value I had. My name.

"My name is Tomás Morín. Mrs. Morín's son."

She nodded and let me through.

My stomach cramped. Did the kid behind me know what had just happened? I would rather have been bobbing in the Gulf being stung by jellyfish than in that cafeteria. I couldn't be sure, but I was grateful my mother had spoken with the lunch lady in time.

That poor, poor mom of mine is what I say now, but who am I kidding? For a long time, I blamed her as much as I blamed my father. Sure, she didn't shoot up like him every other day. In fact, she's never done a drug in her life, but what did I know of codependency and enabling when I was eight? But I was an expert in wants.

I wanted toys.

I wanted food.

I wanted rest.

All in that order, usually. My father in the house made two out of three a challenge.

MY PROUDEST MOMENT of begging as a child came when I convinced my mom to buy me a set of encyclopedias from the man at our door. It didn't matter that he wasn't an official representative of World Book or that a few volumes were missing. When he carried the books out of the trunk of his yellow Lincoln Continental, I just knew the endless questions of my life would finally have answers.

All of the photos inside were black and white, with the exception of a full-color insert of all of the earth's animals. Each page represented a different part of the world. Every time I finished looking something up, I treated myself to the animals flying, swimming, sitting, perching, running in full, deep colors across the page.

Embossed on the cover of each encyclopedia was a small circle about the size of a half-dollar. Inside the circle was a blocky creature that resembled a goblin. With arms and legs extended, it looked like it had been caught in the middle of a jumping jack. For the next twenty years, I believed this was World Book's mascot, until one day the negative image I was seeing flipped and I saw the Western Hemisphere with its beige oceans and gold continents. I miss that happy goblin. He always looked happier than the earth did.

If I wanted Ric Flair's NWA World Championship Belt sold in stores, I made it myself. An afternoon of dumpster diving around town for the most pristine cardboard box was all I needed. And a box of crayons and a black ballpoint pen. My legs hanging out of the dumpsters behind the convenience stores, I hunted for the mint Frito Lay boxes I coveted. Their natural folds lined up with where the belt would wrap around my waist. By the time I was done, I bragged how my belt was better than the official ones at the store.

When I wanted the Super Friends action figures, I turned to poster board. Batman, Wonder Woman, and Superman were easy. Samurai gave me fits, because his legs turned into a tornado. When I realized I could color the negative space between his legs like a funnel cloud and fold it behind him when he walked or fold his legs back when he flew, I was set. The Transformers? A piece of cake after I discovered slots and tabs.

When I saw my first tree house on TV, I was really up against it then. That tree house lived in my dreams more than my own house.

The kid in the movie was the kind I loved to resent, because I was poor and it made me feel better. I told myself a tree house with curtains, a door, and windows would be wasted on a kid like that. He could never appreciate it the way I could. Life had given him everything: a miniature house in a massive oak at the edge of a yard; on the other side of the yard, a white house with green shutters; a kitchen with his mother in her spotless apron, who had cooked a moist roast while his father set the table. After a few minutes, they walked to the window and called their son in for dinner.

How could he be happy? I thought. How could he know how precious his life was if he was never afraid of losing it? Did he ever fantasize about biblical-level floods rising from the highway to swallow up him and his family? I could appreciate what he had more than he ever could. I could be the better son.

Sometimes lies can save us, keep us going when we need it most.

If I could have used poster board for my tree house, I would have. The best I could do was some old wood my father had dropped in the yard and forgotten. When I collected it and sized up what I had, there was just enough to make a floor. Someone I no longer remember helped me lift it into the tree in my backyard. If you looked out the back door, you could've made out my body suspended in the tree. It wasn't all that far away, but it was the first place I could call my own.

Once I secured it in the arms of the tree, I'd crawl up like a lizard and lie on my back with arms spread wide like the man Corpus Christi was named after. Only, unlike him, I gave into my self-pity. I ate it like a bag of cookies, sucking the red, blue, and white stains of its sprinkles off my fingers. I could never get enough. Even when I was bloated with it, I wanted more.

Sometimes I would sleep.

Other times I would cry.

Always I would listen.

From my perch, the silky song of the bamboo forest below, the one place where I could be invisible. Truly invisible. No magic required. Two trails led to where a tree had fallen and begun to rot. Because it didn't fall flush, it made the soft yellow roof of a triangle. While a gentle finger could make the damp bottom flake, the top was dotted with plants whose tiny green bodies stretched toward the little light there was. Curled underneath, I napped and fell out of the world.

Once, I woke confused in my warm black hole and found that the fence of green and yellow around me had gone strange. The wind massaged the bamboo, and my life rushed back.

Dirty and dazed, I walked out and climbed my tree. I closed my eyes and felt the gentle Gulf air warm my face. In two hours it would be dark, and my father's schemes would take flight. A storm churned off the coast. I was as ready as the tree.

THEY CALLED MY father Indio. Well, his friends called him Chief. Even the ones who spoke Spanish. Indio was mostly for strangers or business. One summer, I saw a man call him Chief, and then his mouth twisted into a slice of watermelon.

In first grade, I thought I cracked the mystery of where Indio came from. On the cover of my Big Chief writing tablet, there was my father's dark skin, the furrowed brow. There was even the mix of pride and hurt in his eyes forever fixed on something just over my shoulder.

Though my father's face on everyone's tablets made me flush and beam, I tried to keep it to myself. It wasn't safe to talk about my father at school, because people might ask questions. Even when a bully was in my face or I wanted to impress a little girl, I shut my mouth. If I didn't, then next thing I knew, my classmate with the prettiest pigtails would be at her kitchen table practicing her letters. Maybe that tricky K. Then her father walks in to grab a beer. On his way to the couch to finish watching *Hill Street Blues*, he looks over her shoulder at the row of letters tilted like wooden crosses in a cemetery and says, "That's good, mija."

She smiles and points to my father's face on the cover of her tablet and tells her father a story about the little boy in her class.

Her father laughs as his face wrinkles into a worn baseball glove. "Which little boy?"

"Tomás."

"Tomás who? What's his last name, mija?"

Her tiny shoulders rise to her ears.

"Babe, what's the last name of the boy named Tomás in mija's class?"

Her mother reading in the next room calls out, "Morín. His name is Morín."

"Is his father Joe Morín?"

"Yeah, I think so."

"Mija, I don't want you talking to this boy. His father does bad things."

"What kinds of bad things?"

"You're too little to know. He's like the bad men on daddy's TV show. Promise me you won't talk to him anymore. Okay? Just be friends with other boys."

"Okay, Daddy."

And so it would end. Another little girl whose hand I wouldn't get to hold crossed off my list.

I knew that the things my father did were bad. Being trained to watch for the "evil" police had taught me that. What I couldn't decide was: Did my father do bad things, or was he a bad person? Not knowing made me afraid. If he was a bad person, would people think I was bad too when they found out he was my father?

Left

Right

Left

It was years before I found out the real story behind my father's nickname. When he was born, his family lived in Wyoming. They had migrated, as so many other families did, in search of work. The day his mother gave birth to him, his father showed up to the hospital to ask one question. When he found the nurse, he said, "Is it a boy or a girl?" As the story goes, he got his answer and, without seeing his wife or child, left to smoke cigars and drink with his friends.

When he came back the next day, he asked to see his baby. When he saw how dark his son was, he joked, "No you don't! You're trying to slip me an indio! I know what you're up to!"

The running joke at the time among the migrant workers in Wyoming was that hospitals were trying to find homes for orphaned Native American infants by passing them off as Mexican American babies. Even though the joke was racist, not to mention made no logical sense, the hospital hallway filled with laughter and no one cared. When he looked at his son, he decided to keep the nickname after all, because my father did look like a little indio to him.

ONE OF THE first scents I ever loved was wet cement. Sometimes my father would mix it all up in a wheelbarrow. Sand, water, cement. If he was touching up a house he had built or just starting a new one, he would dump it all inside his mixer and pull it to the construction site.

The mixer was open at the top and shaped like a deep rectangular bowl, unlike the round drums most bricklayers use nowadays. It had two arms along a horizontal shaft on the inside. They would rotate along an axis until all the ingredients had mixed and the cement had gone from clumpy tan to a deep gray. It was the shade of gray you might see on a quilt of storm clouds just before they drop their rain. The cement was cool on the tip of my fingers. It groaned every time my father sliced it with his trowel and pulled away and up the exact amount he needed.

The smell was clean. Not subtle. It's strong in the way cake frosting is strong. As you get closer to it, it moves from itself to your nose quickly, and once it's inside, its sharp, metallic fullness crowds everything else out.

He was an artist. There's no question about that. Stone and women were his medium. And we kids, what were we? Maybe we were the gray sludge that held his families together. We were strong and made each house of love he built stand straight and tall. We would have lasted forever if only he had remembered that nothing lasts forever. Least of all what we build.

My mother's father—the only man I ever called grandpa, or abuelo—was an old-timer who would say, about a man like my father, something like, "El que no mantiene, no detiene." I can hear those words crackle in his mouth. But he'd be wrong. It wasn't a lack of care that made the families my father built crumble, it was the roofs. Or rather, the ones that weren't there. I never did see my father build one. That was for a different crew. You'd think somewhere along the line a person would've told him that a house with no roof is just a box to hold the light.

For all his talent, my father only built my family two things. The first was a short, four-post brick fence. Each post was thick and made from fire engine–red brick. Green metal flares connected one post to another.

The other thing he built was a laundry room for my mom. He started to, rather. After he laid the concrete foundation and collected cinder blocks, that was it. After it sat in our backyard for years, my mom relented to my constant requests to use it as a basketball court. I watched my father, for the last time, mix a small batch of concrete and cement a black metal pole to the center of a large truck tire. When the concrete had dried, I attached my backboard and rim to the pole. With someone guiding the top so it wouldn't hit the ground, I could lean my goal over and roll it anywhere in the yard I wanted.

The railroad worker who owned the house before us had built it with materials that were no doubt free and handy at his work. We discovered this when we busted the front wall in order to move the bedroom door over and found railroad ties instead of two-by-fours.

When hurricanes came over from the Gulf, our house felt like the safest place in Mathis. One day after we had long left the house, fire would claim it. Only the two foundations and the fence posts would be left, their red bricks cracked and crumbling, squat sentinels in the near empty lot.

I admired the houses my father built. I was in awe at how he could take a dull pile of brick and make it a home. Sometimes a family requested stone.

One night, I dreamed I was at his work site. Piles of sand surrounded me. I sat cross-legged, so when I looked around, the shifting points of these pyramids were taller than I was. For a long time, I believed my dream was real, until one day in yoga class I grimaced and remembered how uncomfortable it has always been to sit with my legs folded in front of me.

In the dream, I study the grains of sand. They start their run near the top. It always happens suddenly. You would think a breeze or a fly disturbing the wall of granules would be needed to make it move, but that's not true. The pyramid's contract with gravity has an expiration date, especially when the sand is not packed. Sometimes the grains only make it halfway down the pyramid, while other times a few will build enough speed that their momentum will take them all the way to the leaves of grass and the dirt under them. I stare and wonder how long it would take for every grain to make it to the grass. Would a year be long enough for them to all run away and leave a beige circle where a pyramid had once stood? A year still feels like such a long time.

You can fit so much pain into twelve months.

When my father tosses a stone back into the pile, the knock when it hits the other stones startles me. I've never seen him chop a stone with his trowel the way he will a brick that's too long. A stone fits or it doesn't. When I ask how he knows which stone will be next, he talks about puzzles. In the case of a house, there was no box with a picture to look at. He would look at the space he needed to fill, as well as the ones that didn't exist yet, and stay two or three spaces ahead. I could see those spaces too. I figured everyone could see their unlined shapes, until someone told me most people don't see negative space first.

The stone in his hand is the color of moldy bread. He fits it snug in the wall. Unlike the sand, it won't run. If people live in this house a hundred years and then abandon it for another hundred, it will still sit there with its blue-green eye, unblinking and full of hope.

I WAS IN Chicago for the first (or maybe it was the second) time for a writer's conference. In order to escape the social quicksand of ten thousand writers all poured into one place, my friend Emilia suggested we visit the Art Institute of Chicago. I had never been there, so I was excited by the chance to find some Edward Hoppers, Jackson Pollocks, or Francisco Goyas that I had never seen before. Emilia was hoping to find a Caravaggio, Joseph Cornell, or an Egon Schiele. I had never heard of Schiele, though I loved Caravaggio and Cornell. The museum would be closing soon, so we picked up a map and found someone to help us route what would have to be a quick trip.

We were out of luck with Caravaggio and Schiele. Hopper too. I think *Nighthawks* was traveling or the exhibit was under renovation. I can never remember which. We fared better with Cornell when we found two walls dedicated to his mysterious work. I could hardly believe our luck. The boxes I had seen photos of in countless books were now there, at least three dozen of them in total, sprinkled with bits of night and feathers and all sorts of objects Cornell ran across during his hunt for materials in New York City.

Behind the glass the contents of each box seemed ready to move and enact a drama meant for our eyes and no one else's. Behind the glass, there was another drama orchestrated by the person who had hung each box perfectly parallel to the floor, as well as to every other box, so that the vertical lines invisibly stretching out from each box never crossed the vertical lines of another box and I know this because I counted every LeftRigh-

tLeft LeftRightLeft LeftRightLeft LeftRightLeft LeftRight-
Left LeftRightLeft LeftRightLeft line until I was lost in this
unheralded symphony of symmetry that would go unnoticed
by most everyone who would stand before it, who would only
see a Cornell exhibit. The room felt warm when I saw my face
reflected in the glass. I turned and walked off quickly.

I found Emilia and asked her if we had time to hunt a Pollock
before the museum closed.

In one of the brightly lit rooms upstairs, we looked for *Greyed
Rainbow*, one of three Pollocks the museum owned. When we
found it, at first we didn't think too much of it. Emilia wandered off to see what else was in the room while I stood there
disappointed. I had long loved Pollock's drip paintings. A friend
had pointed out to me once how ironic this was, considering
how much I craved order and tidiness. What I tried to point
out, unsuccessfully, was that his paintings were not full of chaos.
Rather, they were order and intention at their most chaotic. I
wanted to be wild in the same way his drip paintings were.

Before I left to find Emilia, it occurred to me that maybe I had
been standing too close to the six-by-eight-foot rectangle of thick
and thin, flat and textured swirls of gray and black and white.

I moved closer and read the title. I thought of the impression-
ists and how their fields of flowers always looked better from
across the room. When I stepped back far enough, the swatches
of color Pollock had hidden in the negative space of the bottom
third of the painting came alive. One by one, each pulled away
from the canvas and burst out toward me.

orange
  pink
blue
  yellow

My breath caught every time a new color would move toward
me from the canvas and hold there a second so that I could see it

for itself and not just for what it was a part of. While I was caught in my own personal fireworks show, tears pooled in my eyes. Ashamed, I looked away when I remembered what my abuelo had said about men crying in front of others. This painting I had never heard of, by one of my favorite painters, had broken me open. I needed to hide.

In that moment, for no reason I could understand, I thought of my father for the first time in years and regretted that I had stopped speaking to him over a decade ago.

I thought about how if we ever became close again, then I could come back to the museum with him so that he could see *Greyed Rainbow*. We would stand in the gallery full of strangers, side by side, as they buzzed around us. I would even take his rough hand gently in my own and sit us on the floor. We would each cross our legs and stare. He would study the painting as I told him about Pollock's technique, how they both worked with a cigarette dangling from their lips, one dripping cement, the other paint. I would mention Pollock's trouble with alcohol, and the affairs, too. This would endear Pollock to him, would make him one more fellow builder groping for love through the fog of his life.

My father would look at the painting, and I would look at him looking at it. I would study the angle of his knees, and how the cradle of his legs would take the shape of a boomerang that would always come back.

On Names

When I was growing up, you could probably go in many neighborhoods where people were up to no good in the Coastal Bend area and mention El Indio, and if someone didn't know him, they knew someone who did. As far as nicknames go, Indio and Chief are pretty good. What guy wouldn't want to be called Chief?

In Mathis, Texas, many people had nicknames. The one catch was that you couldn't pick your own. If you tried, you'd be ignored and get called by whatever nickname your body suggested. Or worse, some interesting lie about you that was making the rounds.

One guy, everyone called Tick. He was short, overweight, and had the kind of plump, happy face you get after gorging on the neighbor's dog.

Another guy was nicknamed Rana, because he had a voice so raspy it reminded you of a frog croaking. Had Tom Waits been from Mathis, Rana would have had competition for his name.

A group of people could also be given a nickname. Someone walking down the road one day looked in a yard where kids were crawling in a tree like monkeys. That was all it took for those brothers and sisters to be called Los Changos. A pair of brothers from another family were Los Calcetines after someone saw them playing outside as children with nothing on their feet but long socks.

A nickname didn't always end with the person it was given to. When a man named La Víbora had children, it seemed like the most natural thing to call all of his kids snakes too. In conversation, that family was then known as Las Víboras.

If you had been nicknamed La Paca because your long torso with no curves reminded people of a rectangular hay bale, then when you had children who inherited the shape of your body, of course everyone was going to call your kids Las Paquitas.

Physical disabilities were not out of bounds. If I had had a bum leg I dragged behind me, I might've been nicknamed Escoba, because of the sweeping motion my leg made. A boy who was born mute was called Mudo. A man who was my father's age was El Columpio after his legs that had been twisted by polio made him swing his arms and legs when he walked. While calling someone a swing sounds cruel, he smiled when I saw someone yell, "Columpio!" And why wouldn't he smile, when having a nickname meant you belonged? Besides, who wouldn't want people to say your name and think of kids laughing as they swung from the earth to the sky like pendulums of joy?

Happy Families

I felt like a surfer standing inside the dumpster. I tried to tame the trash as it shifted under my small feet so that I could make it over to the two bags I was after. They were clear plastic and bigger than anyone would ever use in their kitchen. Each one had a knot that was like a fist.

They bulged with glazed doughnuts, cinnamon rolls, jelly doughnuts sticking out the tips of their strawberry tongues, long johns with crème filling, apple fritters. My mouth watered. I had tasted them all before. The memories of their flavors made my stomach clench with anticipation.

I handed a bag to my mom. As she helped me climb out, my father kept an eye out for the police. We couldn't let our guard down even on a Sunday morning, when the streets were empty. As my father drove us home, behind the dumpsters near the loading dock of the grocery store, I saw stacks of brown, red, and blue milk crates and wondered: If we could take food we weren't supposed to have, then could I take a crate and finally get the basketball goal I pined for? I decided I would come back later to take one.

At the kitchen table my father opened our treasure. The glaze and chocolate and fruit fillings peeled away and clung to the inside of the bag. Two days before, when I couldn't afford them, I had stared at all of these pastries lined up in their neat rows in cool cases inside the store. Now they were free, and I couldn't bring myself to eat more than one. I had wanted to eat all of them when I was in the dumpster. They were hot now. And the bag was moist with their sweat.

I didn't know it, but already my standards for pastries were recalibrating so that it would be decades before I could buy a doughnut without inspecting its skin for breaks in the glaze. The Sistine Chapel of doughnuts wouldn't be good enough. My lips would not suffer a cracked surface, no matter how fresh the glaze.

When we drove away from the grocery store, I had thought how wasteful it seemed for the store to throw such good food away. We never hunted pastries in the dumpster again. We threw so many of them in our own trash can that my father must have thought the risk of getting caught was too great for so little pay-off. My grandfather liked to say, "Pansa llena, corazón contento." It's true—a full belly can make the heart happy, but the catch is knowing what you're really hungry for.

MY MOM TOWELS my father after a bath. Her hands whir so that I can't make out her delicate fingers. She is like some mythical creature with towels for hands. I don't like seeing him tremble. Even if he is cold, I need to see some strength. Just once. Sure, I have seen him weaker and sicker wearing nothing more than boxers, but there is something about the absence of even a thin pair of underwear that makes him more hopeless than usual. Naked like that with the towel swishing around him, he is like another kid in the family. The last thing I wanted was a brother. Especially one that couldn't even bathe himself.

Growing up, my room shared a wall with my parents' bedroom. I never heard what you probably think I should have. A stomach folding like an accordion was the only music at night in our house. Sometimes we'd run out of money, and he couldn't score. When I heard his song, I went to their door and peeked in. I didn't want to see anyone naked.

When I made out the outline of their nightclothes, I walked in and checked how wet the washcloth on my father's forehead was. It was dry, so I rewet it in the bathroom. I rung it out just enough so that it would still feel cold but not drip and make him shake more. None of us spoke. My mom stood and stretched, then sat to rest as I took a shift and kept his forehead cool and stroked his hair.

We were a makeshift triage in the dark. For years, I believed we both wanted out of that room, but maybe that's not true. Maybe she wanted to be right where she was, with the man she loved, keeping him alive.

I couldn't care less about any of the remote and beautiful places I was reading about in my encyclopedias. I wanted to be in that same room, too, only in the daytime, with the bed made up, the morning light muted through peach lace curtains, cardinals piping their song in from the empty streets. Home from school on a sick day, while everyone was at work, that was my idea of heaven on those shaky nights of sweat and vomit.

When the dry heaves started, my father would say, "Llévame al hospital." When we heard these words, we knew things were serious, because my father hated hospitals.

Without saying a word, we rose in that dark humid room and prepared for the drive to the hospital in Calallen. As she struggled to get some pants on my father, I dressed in my room and then took a pillow and a blanket to the back seat of our car. The only thing left was to help my mom lift him up. Like two human crutches under his arms, we stepped into the cool night.

Left

Right

Left

Whether we drove to the small hospital in Calallen just up the road or trekked all the way into Corpus depended on how recently he'd been sick. Since Calallen was a small operation, there were only so many nurses and doctors who worked the ER. We would get looks if we took my father there too often. And by *we*, I mean my mom and I. If it seemed like he would die before we made it to Corpus, then Calallen it was.

When my mom said my father was sick, it didn't take long for the doctor to figure out that he had withdrawals. Like us, they would pretend that what was happening wasn't really happening, that my father was no different than any other decent, moral, upstanding citizen who had caught a stomach bug. If they pretended to believe that, then it meant we were his loving, loyal family come to the rescue.

Sometimes I felt we were accused of jumping the gun, of not waiting to see if my father would pull through the withdrawals at home and finally kick his habit. I felt relieved when we entered an ER and I didn't recognize the staff. Because the hospital in Corpus was big, we were guaranteed the doctors and nurses would be different. Go to Calallen too many times, though, and sometimes we had to because there wasn't enough gas to make it to Corpus, and those nurses and doctors would be too tired to play their parts. On those nights, their faces were like balloons in a tree.

But there was another look I dreaded more. That face made me feel like an accomplice, like my mom and I were just as guilty as the dealers who sold to my father. That face said, *Why couldn't you take him somewhere else?* or *Not them again. Why did you have to come during my shift?*

What I hated about these looks was not their heartlessness but that I had thought these same things long before they had. I hated them because their hopelessness and impatience were my own. At seven or eight or nine years old, my natural optimism was already warped, because I wanted my father to hurry up and die or just get better already. If he were dead, then at least we'd have peace. And he would too. It would be a win-win, just as if he stopped using drugs and recovered.

The only time I ever sat in the passenger seat when all of us were in the car was during these trips to the hospital. My father in and out of sleep, groaning in the back, for once I was not afraid to look at him. The searching, alien stare he would give me when I did look at him was gone. Now it was my turn to stop counting and stare.

It would be years before I would perplex and irritate the women in my life with my bedside manner when they fell sick. While I was attentive, I was also cold. I would say no soft words to try and ease their discomfort. I did what was needed and little more. It's hard for me to express much for a sick person. My father hadn't needed a son who was scared and crying over his old man's every groan. I learned that my energy was better used for taking care of people. Action, not emotion, is what he taught me.

But all of this was decades away. What I most wanted when I had his attention those nights was to talk. I wanted to tell him about the girl with the chubby cheeks I had a crush on. I needed my father's advice on how to deal with Red, the bully; I wanted to tell him all about my new best friend, Zachary, the kindest person I had ever met.

Instead, I said nothing. I watched and made sure his breathing didn't stop and kept my mom awake so we didn't run off the road.

Left

Right

Left

Right

Left

Right

When we had had too many ER visits in a row and my mom's endless patience ran out, we drove him, against his will, to a rehab clinic. I liked the people there. Their faces never judged us. These people praised my mom's courage and strength. They also told her what she already knew, that she was part of the problem.

As we started on the road back home from either the hospital or the rehab clinic, I was sure of two things. The first was that in a couple of days my father would escape from the hospital or clinic—once with his ass hanging out of his gown—and call us to say he needed a ride home. The other thing I was sure of was that he would live through the night. This meant my mom and I would soon be home and sleeping that sound and enviable sleep of the dead so that by the time the fast-approaching morning came, I would have slept so well it would feel like the light of day had taken years to arrive.

MY FATHER DIDN'T know about Zachary. He didn't know about any of the kids in my elementary school, because I never told him. Not Red, who threatened me with total annihilation. Nor the little girl with chubby cheeks and curly brown hair I had a crush on, the one my abuelo had said was an excellent pick because the little girl's family had a ranch with lots of cattle.

If I had told my father about Zachary, I would have started with Zachary's legs. He was, and still is, the thinnest person I've ever met. Not to mention the palest. He was thin like turkey sliced on a one when you hold it up to the light. His legs were like the new white rope that connected the tetherball to the pole on the playground. When he swung his spindly arm and hit the tetherball, I never once thought he might be trying to take my head off like the stronger kids.

In the herd, we were the weak and pathetic ones. Only, Zachary seemed to not know this in the way I did. Or he knew but didn't care. Maybe his strength came from his sideburns. I've never seen a kid since with facial hair like that. In truth, his sideburns were probably just hair that grew down from his scalp. Sometimes I remember his hair as feathery, and other times I remember it as thick and rough. Always it is blond, like honey in a glass jar.

When he walked, it looked like pulling taffy. A disease had left his legs crooked at birth. Though braces had made them straighter, his knees and feet still turned inward. There was a deliberateness to his walk. He looked like movie cowboys when they grind one step at a time toward each other at high noon. This image unravels if you look at his shoes and realize he walked on the balls of his feet. Never touching the ground, the soles of Zachary's feet must have been soft as butter. Look at his feet and legs and child beard about to connect with his bushy eyebrows, and see what I saw—a boy bent like the sweetest musical note.

I was lucky. Unlike Zachary, I hadn't been betrayed by the world before I was born. I didn't have the fierce face of a wolverine like he did. With my chubby cheeks and vacant eyes, my face resembled a cherub's in the corner of a painting. Little more than ignored decorations with no bows and arrows to shoot people with, it's all those cherubs can do to keep from turning on each other out of boredom.

I wanted to be more invisible, so we tried to master the art of walking quietly. *Like ninjas*, Zachary and I would say. We practiced moving across the playground while crunching the least amount of sand. It was on this playground where he told me he was moving away—his mother had said it was for the best and that he would make new friends.

His words dripped from his lips. He said them like someone who had said these sad words before and had found them to be true. They had a lightness to them. I think it was hope.

Then the bell rang.

The next day, I knew to not look for him at recess.

I spent the rest of that school year alone on the railroad rail that had been repurposed as a balance beam for the playground. Sometimes the ground was lava, and other times, snakes slithered all around me. Again and again I fell into the nest of molten vipers. And when the rail was busy with kids racing their Hot Wheels cars on it, I retreated to the swing and lost myself in that brief second when I would jump just before my swing reached its height and hang between the sky and the earth, not knowing where my feet would land, hearing nothing except the hard pounding of my own heart.

A NEW GRADE meant a new playground. Both the rail and the sand were gone. Now I had trees and monkey bars.

The first time I spoke to Isobel was in the lunch line. About milk, I think, how the small cartons were the same shape as the orange juice. One was white with black writing; and the other, white with orange writing. Aside from the color and the contents, they were the same square with the angled roof you were supposed to fold and dig your finger into. Pull, pucker, and drink.

I was an ace with shapes. I never colored outside the lines. By my estimation, I was already a master with scissors. To violate the shape of anything felt unforgivable. The formula for not doing this was simple.

Pay attention.

Take your time.

Be careful.

That was all it took. I just imagined how I would feel if I were a paper fish that a kid had attempted to color purple by scrawling across me as if his arm were a windshield wiper. If I were that fish, I'd want to know what was wrong with that kid's parents that they didn't teach him about respecting borders. I'd wonder what parts of me I would lose when he picked up his scissors and how I would ever get home to the ocean looking like that.

Isobel was not one of those kids. Her coloring and scissor work were all the proof I needed that she had good parents. Her hair ran in long, even black braids halfway down her back. When we became friends, Zachary had been gone for a year. After we talked about milk cartons, it wasn't long before we'd look for each other on the playground. We talked on the monkey bars during lunch. Before long the other kids sang at us about sitting in a tree and baby carriages. While my face would pink when someone sang it, Isobel would stand and tell them to cut it out. I didn't understand how climbing a tree and kissing could be better than Isobel looking at me and listening. Even Zachary had never really looked at me when I spoke, because like me, he was easily distracted.

My family and teachers all listened when I spoke, but I never felt like any of them paid me any attention. Not like Isobel. She would look at me when I spoke, and as she did, my words moved across her face in squints, blinks, and furrows. It would be years before I realized she was returning the attention I gave her when she spoke, the attention I gave away so freely to anyone and everyone because I didn't know just how much it was worth.

When her head cocked to one side, that was her sign to me that I had gotten distracted. Finding my train of thought, I asked her if she was going to watch David Copperfield that night.

"I don't know. Who's that?"

"He's a magician who does tricks."

"Cool. What kinds of tricks?"

"I don't know. The commercial said he's going to make the Statue of Liberty disappear."

The bell rang, and we agreed to watch the show that night and talk about all his magic tricks.

The next morning, I had my list of theories ready and organized. When we met on the playground, I noticed her smile was missing. She looked at her feet and whispered, "My parents didn't let me watch the magic show."

"How come?" I said. I sat next to her and leaned in so I could hear her better. "What's wrong?"

Tears stumbled down her cheeks. "My parents said I'm a Jehovah's Witness and we don't watch magic."

"Why not?"

"My mom says magic is the devil. And anyone who watches it is a devil worshipper. They said I can't be your friend anymore."

I knew who the devil was. Every good Catholic kid had heard all about him at catechism. David Copperfield was not the evil monster I knew was hiding under my bed at night. I stared at her wet face. Before I could say anything, she looked me in the eye and said, "I'm sorry."

As she rose, my mind raced through all of Copperfield's tricks and the theories I had worked up to explain them. Hidden compartments, springs, a key in his pocket . . . None of it was real magic. I was sure of it. Least of all the Statue of Liberty trick. It had to all be done with mirrors. And lies. There was no other way to explain it. All the theories I had wanted to talk about with her now became evidence we could give to her parents so they could see that Copperfield was not the devil and we could stay friends.

My tongue was in a straitjacket. There were chains over it and no key in sight. I watched her walk away, my feet in cement.

Even though we never spoke again, the next few weeks, I searched the dictionary and my encyclopedias to try and understand what a Jehovah's Witness was and how they could think David Copperfield was the devil. How could this skinny guy with the tan and bushy eyebrows, with the pleated pants and the cape, be the lord of all evil? There was no way he could fit his chicken foot in his boots. The goat hoof I could understand, but the chicken foot? Impossible.

My parents were no help. Nobody in my neighborhood knew a Jehovah's Witness either. Apparently, I was the only person who had ever met one. Riding my bike by their temple revealed no clues either. They were tall and short, sometimes both in one family. They wore shirts and dresses and pants and shoes. All of them with two legs and two arms. Where did they hide their fear of magic? The people who entered and left their temple looked like everyone else in town.

In another year or two, Isobel was gone, her family moved to who knows where. I held out hope that her family was simply homeschooling her, but after a while, that hope faded too. Soon Jehovah's Witnesses began to visit my neighborhood. The first morning I met them, I wondered whether Isobel's parents had discovered where my family lived and put our names at the top of the list of their outreach program since we were, no doubt, a nest of devil worshippers.

When they knocked on our door and identified themselves, I happily accepted their offer to come in and discuss the Word with me. They came in, oblivious to the fact that I was only eight and my parents were nowhere to be seen. My parents were still asleep in the next room, on account of it being Saturday, not to mention Friday had included the usual long, late drive to Corpus so my father could score.

Left

Right

Left

The two men in starched shirts and ties sat on my couch talking about the ministry of Jesus, their back issues of the *Watchtower* in my hands. Their Jesus looked like the Jesus I had seen growing up. He had the same flowing brown hair, loose robe, and patient eyes. He looked like the kind of person who could sit and hear you tell the longest story and be happy he had.

In spite of my deep interest in the Bible—I had spent a lot of time reading my grandparents' giant, illustrated copy—I most wanted to know about Isobel. When they asked me if I believed in God, I wanted to say, "Isobel's hair looks like black cinnamon twists."

"Do you know that Jesus and the archangel Michael are the same?"

"Isobel's plaid shirts are nice. The black-and-red one is my favorite."

"Do you know that we are living in the last days?"

"Isobel and I never got to talk about prophets. John the Baptist is my favorite. He kept talking after everyone stopped listening. Do you know her family?"

That last question is the one I most wanted to ask but never did. I was too afraid that if I was already a devil worshipper in their eyes, then showing I was more interested in a girl from their congregation than in the kingdom of heaven might mean they would never visit my house again. And if this were to happen, then the last, slight connection to Isobel would be broken, and my chance of her ever knocking on my door to preach the Word would be gone. For the next couple of years, I placed all my hope on pulling a clue out of those Saturday morning conversations about my friend. Instead, I only found news about hope and forgiveness.

I WOKE STARTLED from a nap. After I caught my breath, I climbed the eucalyptus tree in the front yard. The stump of this tree was wider than our car and taller than a basketball rim. The crook in each of its arms was more comfortable than any chair we owned. My tiny legs hung around the massive limb that had once risen high into the air. It was my wooden elephant.

From its back, my corner of the neighborhood stretched out in all directions. I could breathe and my mind could be still for once up there. I ran my fingers across its rings and thought about how it had been with me my whole life. Once, I attached a handle to the inside of a piece of its fallen bark and used it as a shield when I played war. I missed the days before it had been broken, when I would tilt my head back and try to follow its long limbs to their sharp ends far into the sky, until I could feel my heart beating on the side of my head and the clouds started turning circles and I would almost fall.

When storm winds broke a massive branch that almost hit our roof, the neighbors were called to bring a chainsaw. The decision was made to cut down not just the eucalyptus in front but the one in back too. No one seemed sad about this, maybe because the trees had been dead for so long. In spite of this, they had refused to fall in the way that my father's sick, worn-out friends were doing. When my abuelo met people like them, he often said, "Al perro más jodido se le cargan las pulgas." And he was right, because wasn't it true that more fleas hitched rides on the most hopeless dogs?

The men who were going to cut down the tree in the front yard quickly learned the chainsaw was useless. If the tree had been hollow, twelve people could have packed inside it like sardines. Axes were out of the question, because no one had a week or more to hack away at it. Someone thought setting it on fire might work, but it was too close to our house to chance. Finally, someone suggested wrapping a chain around the tree and pulling it down with a truck.

After everyone cleared out of the way, the truck pulled and pulled. Just when the limb started to bend, the chain broke and the truck lunged forward like a toy. I laughed when everyone gasped and groaned. While someone left to hunt a fatter chain, everyone talked about the tree's strength and how sad it would be when it broke. What saddened me was that no one could remember it alive, which meant no one knew what had killed it.

I had always wondered if it had suffered or gone peacefully or if it had fought the way its lifeless body was fighting now.

Since no one knew the truth, I made up stories about the tree's end. In one story, the tree froze to death during a rare icy winter. Another day, I imagined that all the tree's leaves had once been island birds that had been punished for flying too far from home. One hot summer, a wet breeze from the Gulf blew in the smell of fish and sand and the soft swish of palm trees. When this breeze reached the leaves, they transformed back into birds and flew home, leaving the tree to die.

When someone showed up to my house with a chain fatter than a rattlesnake and ten times as long, I knew the tree's long, elegant arms would do what they had never done before: touch the ground. Each time a limb cracked, it sounded like a rifle. All that was left once everyone was gone was a giant stump for me to perch on that night and dream about the different ways my family's story might end.

By the time the men had finished turning the giant limbs into firewood with their axes and chainsaw, the sun had set, and so the eucalyptus in the backyard would have to wait until tomorrow.

Over the next few days, either the person with the truck was busy or the chain was in use somewhere. In time, everyone forgot about the tree in the back. Even though I couldn't climb this tree, I was joyful it still stood, because it meant when the geese returned from the most northern parts of Canada, their roosting spot would be undisturbed. I knew little about Canada back then, and so the geese were mysterious to me. Had I known they flew from the marshes and ponds of Queen Maud Gulf, Prince Regent Inlet, and the Gulf of Boothia, I would have woven these exotic-sounding places into stories about the realms of geese. They wore brown coats and white collars like the priest at church. With their odd clothes and lonely *huh-gonks*, they were so different from the lumbering, earth-bound white goose we owned, which would patrol our yard and honk angrily at us if we came near it.

Because I was lonely and sad, the songs of those geese sounded lonely and sad to me. I only heard their songs for a few more years before the fat chain and the big truck and the chainsaw would reunite the men of the neighborhood and the last of my two giants came down.

For all I know, the geese that now flew past our house probably trumpeted songs of joy and praise, songs about the escape from their frozen land, about how the warm air of their Texas homes felt deep between their feathers. There were probably songs about goslings, too, and food, and about flying under the moon like one of hope's perfect arrows.

IF YOUR PARENTS do drugs and one of them wants to keep up appearances, then you know the rule: friends from school don't come over. Unless their parents do drugs too. Those friends are okay. My mom was too afraid my school friends would see my father sick or, worse, shooting up. If this got back to their parents, then before we knew it, the police would be at our door, and everyone would know the town's worst-kept secret: my mom, a college-educated woman from a respectable family, had chosen to make a life with a handsome, charismatic drug addict.

Enter Roy and Anna Bowman. My parents had met them the year before I was born. Their daughter, Haley, was a year younger than me. She was as tough as she was pretty. Her hair was the color of wet sand. One Fourth of July, she asked me to hold a lit Black Cat. When it exploded before I could toss it, she laughed at my black-and-red fingers. She played the role of the tough, scrappy boy I wanted to be better than I ever could, the boy who was more like my half brothers, the sons I was convinced my father loved more because they were more like him.

Haley's younger brothers were nicknamed Bobo and Buddy. Bobo's hair was so blond it was almost white. He was thin and wore round glasses. The frames were a gray plastic and wide as popsicle sticks. Buddy was the youngest. He was one year older than my little brother. Buddy's hair was the color of straw when it sits in the sun for too long. He was like a bowling ball with a smile.

Since Roy and Anna did drugs, too, I could play with their kids and not have to hide anything. We all lived the same life of long hunts for drugs that would take us away from home and our friends. When they came over, we played while our parents, with the exception of my mom, got high. Heroin, Big Red soda, and fajitas sizzling in the backyard was a happy weekend.

Only one letter with a hooknose separates *friend* from *fiend*. Everything else unites them. Some people can seem like both, a fiend and a friend. Fiends like the hurt in others, whether it's of their own making or not. They find you the way a fly sniffs out a wound. Who can say what makes one person drawn to another in friendship? When it happens, it's like joining the ends of a cut wire. Would my little brother and I have been friends with Haley, Bobo, and Buddy if we had met at school and didn't have the drug addictions of our parents to bond over? I hope so, but I can't be sure. Scattered across different grades, who knows if we would have ever found each other? I wonder if for some people making a new friend is like buying shoes. You try them out, and if they fit, you get them with the understanding you just added something that suits you and that will wear out one day.

As a kid, I took good care of my shoes, getting more years out of them than should have been possible. I wore them until they no longer fit, and then I wouldn't want to pass them along to my little brother, because I knew you'd be able to see his foot through a hole in the bottom in no time flat.

I had this one pair of black cowboy boots that couldn't have been more than twelve inches tall. I think they had red flames shooting up and down the sides. I kept that leather so clean it shined. A few months after my brother had been wearing them all up and down the block, one of the soles was cracked and the other was so loose it would clap every time he took a step.

One day when I was at my grandparents' house, my then five-year-old brother walked to where I was hunched over in a chair and kicked me in the throat. He never said a word, not when he swung that little leg of his with my boot on the end of it as hard as he could into my Adam's apple nor when I stumbled around, one hand on my neck, the other reaching for his throat.

When the Bowmans stayed the whole day at our house, we would sometimes play war in the empty lot across the street. It was half the size of a city block and covered in brush. A dead-end street bordered one side; the railroad tracks, the other. Being near the middle of town, the lot was like an island where we could escape and lose ourselves in a happy world of pretend knives and bullets that killed you but never made you bleed.

During one game, I jumped out from a hole and surprised Buddy. He yelled and ran. As I chased him, he looked at me over his shoulder and laughed and tried to run faster. Chasing after him, I drew my bow and shot him square in the back with the bow and arrow we had all made together. While the arrows were little more than blunt sticks, I was nine and he was only four. I was startled by the cry that sprang from his little body before he fell to the ground in tears.

The game was over.

I helped him up, and we all walked back to my house, his brother, Bobo, comforting him. My mom was upset and wanted to know why I had shot Buddy in the back. I didn't know. His father said, "Boys will be boys," as Buddy fell into his mother's arms. My father asked what was wrong with me and sent me to my room. I had twisted Buddy's happy face into an awful mask of pain, and there was nothing I could do to change it.

In a year, my mom would kick my father out, and he would never come back. We saw the Bowmans in town once or twice, but it wasn't the same anymore. The hunt for drugs no longer brought us together. Heroin had been the center our joy and pain circled. With my father gone, there were no more good times with them, only the memory of our families laughing together.

I can still see Bobo's finger slide his glasses back up his short nose. His eyes are like blue bonnets in the dark. They search my face for answers, for why I hurt his brother. I wonder if he saw what took me years to learn, that a part of me was hard and had learned how to hurt, that I was not a good boy anymore, not like him.

I'VE JUST TURNED forty and lost count of how many times I've taught the play *Medea*. As usual, my students are stunned by the story of a woman so lost in grief and anger that she could murder her own children.

As I walk home from campus, the sound of crowing drifts toward me through the central Texas night. I don't have a sense of what direction it comes from until I've passed the loud bar. A block later, I hear it again. It comes from one block over, where the street is still lined with houses and not giant apartment complexes.

The road outside my apartment had been under construction for the better part of a year. The city brought in the big diggers to tear the roads up, so what was supposed to be a two-way street was converted to one way while they did their work. Walking to work every morning on a road that was different than what it looked like the day before made it impossible to

Left

Right

Left

with any kind of consistency. The physical world around me kept changing in an unpredictable way, and I couldn't keep up.

I've heard people say that the city was putting in sidewalks, while others said that it was new water mains. The cement pipes as big around as old Volkswagen Beetles sitting by the side of the road were proof enough of the second theory.

Watching the big equipment move around when someone with a lot of experience was behind the controls wasn't much different than watching a ballet dancer that answers to Cat, if they were painted yellow and black and weighed upward of twenty thousand pounds.

There was one front-end loader that I only ever saw one man sitting in. He couldn't have been more than five foot three. His hair was gray, and he was probably in his fifties. I looked for him when I walked down that street on my way to the campus of Texas State, because everything about his face reminded me of my father, whom at the time I hadn't seen for over fifteen years, and his family.

This man had high cheekbones, dark skin, a sharp nose, and the severe gleam I've seen in my father's eyes that speaks to a single-minded, relentless drive to see a thing done once it's started. Many times, I wanted to walk up to this construction worker, ask his name, and find out if he was a distant cousin.

During all the months of construction, I never saw this man talk to a single person. While all the other workers sometimes joked in passing, or gathered in small groups, I never saw him do that once. And maybe it was just bad timing on my part when I happened to walk by, but I can't say I ever saw him smile either.

When he sat at the controls of that front loader, there is only one word that can properly describe him.

Beautiful.

Most of the front loader drivers I've seen approach a pile of sand or gravel at a slow, measured pace and pause for a second, as they get the bottom of the bucket angled just right. Then they pause again once it's loaded and lifted into the air, before they turn around and make their way carefully to the dumping spot.

Not this man. He would charge a pile of gravel, as if to run over it, and while moving fast, he would simultaneously lower his bucket so that the second he reached it, the teeth of the bucket were already digging right in. His dig and scoop were one fluid movement. As he lifted the bucket, he'd also be backing up, so by the time the full bucket was in the air and in front of him, he'd already be flying forward.

That front loader with him on top of it moved the way a living thing does. When I noticed that no one else ever moved the other machines that fast, I realized he was doing it, not to save time, but because he could.

I never knew I could find so much grace and joy in someone moving dirt two hundred feet.

One day, I stopped seeing him around. I looked for him on top of the front loader, but there was someone else there. At first, I worried that he was sick, but then lots of new faces appeared once the road project moved into the last stage. They probably didn't need him anymore now that the hard work was done, so they pulled him and brought in someone green who just wanted to earn a paycheck without running anybody over. I liked to think of him off somewhere in another part of Texas, with a new crew, sitting on top of a fat, shiny front loader, making it dance like a bee that's crazy for spring and its sweetness.

I keep hearing the rooster crowing. I know which house the crowing must come from, even though I have only seen chickens in its yard.

He crowed again, louder this time. His voice is sharp now, like a steam whistle. He is not young but not past his prime either. His throat cuts through the purple night. For no logical reason I can explain, I'm positive his feathers are the same color as the dark when the university and all of its light is at my back and I've started the long climb home up the hill where long hours of counting and ordering wait for me. And his comb, that floppy crown of pride, it is the shiny red of the first tooth that ever squirmed out of my mouth.

It's been a week as I walk by the house where I've seen the hens, and suddenly there he is. When I see him with his two ladies, I realize why I hadn't noticed him before. He is not much bigger than them. Short, rust and black, with a round chest, he is not the jet-black singer of my imagination. He does not have the long, lean bodies of the athletes my father took me to see at a cockfighting farm when I was a kid. This rooster has never lived one leg chained to a pole next to the metal triangle he calls home. He is a father and a partner, a protector and a companion, much like my abuelo's rooster.

My abuelo's chickens terrified me when I was a kid, because I had seen them peck his hands when he was handling them. He was rough with everyone, animals included. They let him know this any way they could. If only making him bleed would have gotten his attention, he might have been kinder.

Dolores Vela Quintana. This is my abuelo's name. Or it was. How can a dead person's name be past tense when their name still lives in your mouth?

Dolores is a reluctant name. It's not like Luis or Juan, the names of his brothers, which leap into the air. Whenever I say his name aloud, it hides in the corners of my mouth.

Un dolor is Spanish for "a hurt." *Dolores* is the plural and means "sorrows" or "pains." Once, he accidentally cut his hand with an electric saw and didn't say a word. Another time, I noticed bruises on his arms. I should've asked him whether he could feel pain, because I never saw him wince. Maybe he was pain.

I did see him cry once, near the end of his life. My abuela and he were arguing like they usually did, and he started weeping and said, "Ya déjame en paz." My abuela's name was Victoria, but I think she felt like she was the one who lost that day.

Vela means "candle." Whether you make the sound of the *V* by biting your bottom lip or by pressing your lips together flat and firm, the end is always the same: your open mouth filled with light.

Quintana can either refer to "the fifth" something or, in archaic Spanish, to "a five-day fever." In seventeenth-century Spain it wouldn't have been uncommon to hear, "Is Diego still sick? Let us pray that his quintana breaks by tomorrow."

During World War I, an American Red Cross worker wrote, "One can only conjecture as to whether the quintan fever described by Hippocrates, Galen, and Razes was the disease known to-day as trench fever."

I am the grandson of Sorrowful Candle of the Five-Day Fever. The flame of his mind was quiet, until it touched his breath and rose like a bright bull that remembered it wasn't dead yet.

Feeding the chickens and hunting eggs were part of my chores when I visited my grandparents. I loved everything about the chickens, from the variety of their voices to the confidence they carried themselves with. The only time I hated being around them was when it was time to clip their wings. When their feathers grew long enough, the chickens flew into the tree above their corral to sleep. I think the dark felt safer from up there.

During clipping time, my job was to hold a chicken steady. Every time was the same. I squat down, and she hangs across my thigh. When I stroke her head, she closes her eyes. My abuelo fans her wing. In his hand are the scissors he uses for cutting metal. Her voice sounds like a coffee maker when it clears its throat to percolate. His eyesight has been getting worse. She scratched his hand when he picked her up. Her chest is hot against my leg. The riffle of a deck of cards, and her feathers float to the ground.

His scratches are bleeding.

The noon sun makes the dull scissors bright. He fans her other wing. The rooster stares and clucks, while the other hens pretend not to notice.

I will look up *cataract* in the dictionary soon.

He holds the tin snips too close to her skin. I can hear someone chewing celery. The dirt is red and brown.

The definition of the word *scream* makes no mention of chickens. I am doing a bad job when she thrashes, he says.

We let her go and she runs away.

That night, she and her sisters slept on the earth with the rest of us. My little brother once saw a dog bite the comb clean off a rooster's head. He stumbled, and then the memory goes blurry.

I haven't roosted in a tree in twenty-five years. I shuffle and shuffle the past, and it comes up hearts every time.

On Being

Smack. Dragon. Tar. Brown Tape. Junk. White Nurse. Henry. Dead on Arrival. Hairy. Chinese Red. Salt. Dirt. Diesel. Joy Flakes. Nice and Easy. Rush Hour. Charley. Blue Bag. H. Good Horse. Antifreeze. Noise. Foil. Hero. And the list goes on. I can't remember what name my father and his friends used. Chiva, maybe.

They say upward of seven hundred thousand people abuse heroin in the United States every year. How can they even know that? I don't recall anyone asking my father to participate in a drug census back when he was using. It has to be over a million, at least.

Any number higher than a hundred can be hard to wrap your mind around. I might as well tell you seven hundred thousand people wrestle alligators every year. It wouldn't mean much more or less if I did.

No matter how hard we try, there are some things the brain can't take in all at once. Even the mathematical genius who carries one hundred thousand digits of pi in his mind can't take in the totality of all those human veins used as tunnels. And if you factor in not just the seven hundred thousand faces of the users but also all the faces of their families and friends, then you'd fail. And even if you could sit there like Haraguchi, the current pi record holder, and call up seven hundred thousand tormented faces, why would you?

If a number that's too big to wrap your mind around isn't bad enough, the word is that heroin is now so pure you don't even need to cook it anymore. Now if you want to bypass the whole business of needles, you just snort it and board a bullet train to oblivion.

> I love thee to the depth and breadth and height
> My soul can reach, when feeling out of sight
> For the ends of being and ideal grace.

This sounds like oblivion to me. What else do you call the place where being and ideal grace come to an end? I've heard some people say heroin is the purest form of love. Self-love, maybe. Users claim that it has the power to make every pain in their life disappear briefly. Of course, every person and joy in their life disappears too. While Elizabeth Barrett Browning was writing these words from "How Do I Love Thee?" to her future husband, this poem always makes me think of my father when he was happy, when he was one of seven hundred thousand souls without a name, and how maybe, just maybe, he might not have felt alone then.

Quiet Need

I love thee to the level of every day's
Most quiet need, by sun and candle-light.

When my elementary teacher passed out the Troll Book Club
flyers, my mind jumped. I couldn't wait to see the new *Heathcliff*
for sale. Even though I knew there would still be no money to
buy me a book, just like the previous month, and the month
before that, I took the flyers home every time. I liked to read the
teasers, study each new cover. I could spend hours stretched out
on the sofa, our black cat, Charlie, in my lap, making up stories
for what happened inside the new *Peanuts* or *The Berenstain Bears
Go to Camp*.

Sometimes I wondered how my family's life would have been
different if we had been animals instead of humans. I can see my
family's new lives in bright colors drawn on sheets of paper as thin
as onion skin. Which book would children love more because it
reminds them most of their own families?

The Morín Seahorses Make More
Mama Seahorse lays 400 eggs in Papa Seahorse's pouch.
He grows like a balloon and is sad before he squeezes
them out and they float away so he can play his trum-
pet long and loud . . .

The Morín Catfish Catastrophe
Papa Catfish has a nursery in his mouth. 1, 2, 3, he wants
to eat. 4, 5, 6, the babies wait and wait to swim. 7, 8, 9,
ready or not, it's time to dine . . .

The Morín Woodpecker Headaches
Mama Woodpecker deep in a tree, f-e-e-d-i-n-g. First
comes love, then come babies, then comes Papa ham-
mering a hole for another Mama's baby carriage . . .

IT'S FAMILY PICTURE DAY, so my mom, her siblings, and my
grandparents are all gathered in my aunt's living room. My grandparents sit while everyone else rotates in and around them. I lean
against my grandmother while my mom stands behind them, one
hand on each of their shoulders. The white buttons of her light-
blue, short-sleeve button-down shirt are bright. Her black hair
parts down the middle and sweeps back into a loose ponytail. A
small gold cross hangs around her neck. I am five or six, which
means my mom has just completed college.

In spite of the years of struggle with my father, she stands
proud and strong in the photo.

Tiny purple polka dots cover my grandmother's lilac blouse.
Her black hair puffs out. The anxious look on her face and the
hint of a smile make me think she's worried she won't smile
at the right time. My mom feels the same way every time a
camera is pointed at her. I wear a pale-green turtleneck with a
dark-green car on the front. Something crawls out from under
its raised hood. Together, the four of us make an almost perfect

equilateral triangle. A pure symbol of symmetry if there ever was one.

Behind us the white wall is decorated with portraits of two butterflies, a jaguar, a cheetah, and what might be a four-point buck. It's impossible to be sure, since only half of its face is visible.

The jaguar looks sleepy, but rather than lazing in a tree, it has been painted sitting in yellow savannah grass. At first glance, the cheetah painting seems to be of only one cheetah, painted from the neck up and floating against a pale-white background. Look closer and you can see there are two cheetahs, one overlaid against the other. The cheetah painting looks a lot like the two-faced portraits that were popular during the eighties. If my mom were not standing behind my grandparents, it would be clear whether this was the same cheetah but from two different angles.

The buck stares straight at the camera from its frame. Between it and the cheetahs, a gold-brown metal sculpture of butterflies climbs the wall.

This menagerie is not the only odd thing in the scene. My grandfather wears a corduroy blazer, a white polo with pink stripes buttoned to the top, and a felt cowboy hat the color of river clay. He has given his hat his version of a cattleman's crease. There is a sling around his arm that is in a cast. While cutting some boards at our house with a circular saw, he sliced the area between his thumb and index finger down to the bone. There was blood and a look of disappointment on his face, because now the work he was doing would have to wait until he recovered from his injuries or, worse yet, until someone completely incompetent finished it.

It's hard to tell what pained him more, sawing his hand open or being posed for pictures.

People come in and out for the pictures but his expression never changes. For all any of us know, he is enduring this indignity by reciting in his head all of his favorite sayings.

Este mundo da vuelta
The world spins

La zorra nunca se ve la cola
The fox never sees its tail

Borrega en el cielo, agua en el suelo
Sheep in the sky, rain on the ground

Quiere tapar el sol con un dedo
He wants to cover the sun with a finger

El que es buen juez por su casa comienza
A good judge begins at home

El muerto y el arrimado a los tres días apestan
A corpse and a visitor smell after three days

Menos burros, más helotes
Less donkeys, more corn

Es candil en la calle y oscuridad en su casa
He's a lamp in the street but darkness at home

Del arbol sale la estilla
The splinter comes from the tree

Hablo de su vida y no de su muerte
I speak of his life and not of his death

THE SQUEAKY HONK of my grandfather's pickup outside broke the Saturday morning silence. While I was disappointed to leave my cartoon, we had a job that wouldn't take more than an hour. Plus, he promised there was a Barq's and a Frito pie for me at the end of it. I had never turned down a Frito pie, especially from Nu Way, where the convenience store clerk would cut open a bag of Fritos along its side and then pour chili and cheese in it.

Mathis had no finer dining in my book.

Just a block from my house, we pulled in front of a mobile home. The old woman who lived there was friends with my grandparents. The job seemed simple enough: remove the giant weeds in a deep ditch out front. When my grandfather didn't pull from his truck a pair of garden shears, I realized the plan wasn't to chop the parts of the weeds grown past the water that had collected after a recent rain.

I disliked getting wet. No, I hated it. Still do. Like a cartoon cat, I stared at the pool of warm, dirty water.

My grandfather placed a hoe in my hands and sat on his tailgate. His cigarette bounced on his lip like a diver testing a board before a jump. My instructions were to stand in the water and carefully rest the blade of the hoe against the thick base of each weed and then, in short, controlled strokes, chop it loose and pile it on the ground above me.

There was no backing out now. My fate had been sealed when I had agreed to the work in exchange for a root beer and a Frito pie that became less and less appetizing with every passing minute.

I considered using tears to weasel out of the deal, but I knew the price would be my grandfather seeing me as not just weak but untrustworthy. Even worse, he might think I was just like my father. Getting wet and keeping my word seemed like a good trade-off, if it meant putting off my greatest fear that any day now I would become my father.

Waist deep in the ditchwater, I made the weeds dance with my hoe. In my mind, I was in one of the Greek myths I loved, a reluctant Hercules bumbling his way through one of the twelve labors. One of my arms was human, the other was half garden implement.

As I laid the first stalks on the ground, I brushed fire ants from my arm. When the next clump of weeds fell, my thigh burned. Ants dotted the surface of the water. Their wet, tiny little mouths communicated to me their fear and anger. When I asked my grandfather if I could climb out because ants were biting me, he took a drag, blew a long cloud of smoke, and said, "Móchale más pronto."

I hacked so fast that laughter billowed out of my grandfather in white clouds. After the last weed floated to the top, I climbed out and brushed all the ants off my legs. I raked the water with my hoe until all the weeds were out and the surface was clear. The job was finally finished. My grandfather stopped smiling when he saw the damage the ants had done to my skin.

"Porque no me dijites que te estaban mordiendo tanto?"

Afraid I was in trouble for not telling him what had been happening to my legs, all I could think to do was shrug.

He hugged me and said, "Mijo es hombre."

That moment, when he called me a man for the first time, rippled far into the future when I refused to cry at his funeral, when for years I would let my depression go undiagnosed and cripple me emotionally. When he dropped the word *hombre* into the lake of my life, its rings spread silently into a future I couldn't imagine.

Hombre.

Man.

Pain.

Alone.

That was the moment those words became synonyms.

Only now do I understand the real lesson I missed that afternoon. That lesson was carried in the sorrow of my grandfather's voice, in his regret that I hadn't spoken up so he could have helped me. I couldn't see as a child that while he prized a person who could go it alone, the real gift is giving those who care about you a chance to help you when you need it most. I thought I was a strong, stubborn weed. The truth is I was an ant all along that had forgotten it was an ant.

The next day at his house, I joined him on the back porch. He always rested on the Sabbath, refusing to even drive. We sat and watched as the church of summer quietly set the world on fire all around us.

MY GRANDFATHER AND I were suckers for westerns. We loved *Gunsmoke* and *The Rifleman* and anything John Wayne. My grandfather found his childhood in these shows, a simpler life filled with cattle and ranches and struggle. In every episode, right was right and wrong was wrong.

Because of these shows, he showed me how to lasso when I was seven. When I learned how to rope a sawhorse, I graduated to practicing how to draw a gun. I studied the hands of the fastest shooters in the movies. When my grandfather said, "Enséñame Matt Dillon," I tightened my holster and did my best impersonation of the six-foot-seven sheriff of *Gunsmoke*.

My stance wide, I fixed my eye on an invisible bad guy. We stepped one foot at a time toward each other, our eyes locked, as the scared sun watched our showdown from behind a cloud. My grandfather's hoarse laugh filled the air when I drew my pistol and shot the villain dead.

I had no idea it was so easy to be a hero.

When I was five, my grandmother bought me a swimming pool. It was baby blue, and fish drawn in different shapes and sizes swam along the bottom. One summer afternoon, my grandfather set the pool under a tree. As he filled it with water, I stripped to my underwear and gathered my toys. Once I was in, I was not supposed to leave.

My grandfather warned me to not make the water dirty by stepping in and out. I nodded and made my action figures dive to the studded bottom. A few minutes later, I was in the house hunting a toy I had forgotten. On my way back to the pool, my grandfather reminded me from the porch about tracking dirt into the water. I apologized and stepped back in to play.

A few minutes later, I was back from the house with another toy. I put my foot in the water and stared at the bits of dirt and grass that floated away from my leg. Over my shoulder, I saw my grandfather stand and uncoil his new bullwhip. My aunt had bought it for him during a trip she took to Mexico. It was brown and white, and the leather, softer than a peach. When she presented him the whip, he remarked how he now had a way to protect the cats from the stray dogs that roamed the neighborhood.

I dropped my toys and ran.

As he walked toward me, the bullwhip trailed him through the grass like a snake. The snake wrapped around my ankle, and I was on the ground. Or my wet feet slipped on the grass. The snake flew high. The snake was a part of his arm. And then it wasn't. The grass against my face for once didn't itch. That day I put my screams somewhere safe, like lucky pennies. But I forgot my pockets had holes, and so I wouldn't find them later.

"¡Te dije que no metieras basura en el agua!" he said.

Three perfect lashes across my back, and the snake went back to sleep. My grandmother called him a savage and took me in the house, where I told her and my mom why he had hit me. They tended the welts on my back like the furrows in someone else's field.

This is an old story.

My grandmother, a city girl at heart, explained that my grandfather was from the country, where they acted like animals, where he and his brothers had been struck with whatever might be close by, like a rope or belt or even a branding iron.

When I stopped crying and my bandages were set, my grandfather asked to speak to me. On the porch he apologized and said I should not have been surprised by what happened, because he had warned me. For some reason I wasn't scared, and so I hugged him. I said I understood, because I did. Cause and effect had never been explained to me in so simple a way.

The next two weeks, as my wounds healed, they reminded me of how much I loved it when he would place his big warm hand on my back. When we hugged, he had promised to never use the whip on me again. I was sure he never would, because he was nothing if not a man of his word.

FROM UNDER MY grandfather's bed, I watch my grandmother's feet appear and disappear as she walks through his room to the bathroom and back.

Her slippers, her feet, each leg is heavy with the weight of her thyroid's failure. She would never know of the little death of that little organ, a death that would one day swell in my mom's throat, bloom in my own, and send out the seeds of our own destruction.

But that is decades away.

My mom is still tall and lean. Her body has not betrayed her yet. I am four and almost too big to fit under the bed. But I still do, and so I am in my favorite place in my favorite room of my grandparents' house. The edge of my grandfather's blanket is the screen between my eyes and the world of feet. Its long fringe is ropey and the green of iceberg lettuce.

This is where I sleep. This is where I dream until I'm too wide to curl on my side, and then I move to the top of the bed, from where I look out the window at the leaves of the mesquite tree slow dancing with the wind.

When my grandparents are dead and I am gone, and grown, and all I can hear is the rattle of the world, on those days, I close my eyes and I am back in that room, watching the dance outside the window, my eyelids, the red of my grandfather's cigarette. My shallow breath is the first note of a song about heartbreak, the soul, and a dove's lonely cry. My grandmother will lullaby that cry to me every time I am sick or hurt as a child. She will pucker her mouth into the great Lola Beltrán's long, and slow, *cucurrucucuuuuuuuu, no llores palooooo-ma-aaaaaa-aaaa-aaa.*

When the world has not been gentle with me, sometimes I sit on my grandfather's lap.

"Me haces una paloma, buelito?"

He nods and takes the last drag of his cigarette. Stamping it out on the arm of his chair, he peels away the paper on the end, and once the filter is free, he pinches it off. With the tips of his fingers, he pulls away the strands from the top of the filter, and then the bottom, until in the palm of his hand sits a tiny white dove. To me it was always a dove, though it looked more like a moth.

I jump off his lap and pretend my dove can fly. I carry it around the yard and imagine it flying over the fence and into the pila next door. The pillar was shaped more like a granary, though there was no grain in sight. Inside, there were only leaves and air so crisp and moist it felt and tasted like what I thought new air would taste like, if there was such a thing. If the pillar were flared at the top, instead of flat, it would look like a miniature nuclear tower.

When I'm tired as a child, I sit across from my grandfather on the porch and ask him to tell me my favorite of his stories, "La Bomba Atómica." Because in Spanish when a vowel occurs at the end and beginning of two words in the way that the *a* does in the middle of "Bomba Atómica," you drop the vowel in the second word. My grandfather would call this his story about "La Bomba Tómica." He would play on the word *tómica*, which is almost a perfect homonym of *tónica*. As a result, the title "The Atomic Bomb" took on a dark irony when it was made to sound like "The Tonic Bomb," an invention that would cure us all.

I never found out when he first made up this story, but if he had known it long before he told it to me during the early eighties, it took on a deeper resonance for me within the context of the

Cold War and the fear I shared with many of my classmates that the Soviets would rain nuclear missiles down on us.

In his story, Coyote travels the world to gather the feces of different kinds of animals in order to create a bomb that would destroy the world once and for all, a world he could no longer control. My favorite part of the story was the roll call of animals Coyote tracked down. My grandfather would start with the domestic animals, the dog and cat, and then move to the animals I would sometimes see on the country roads outside of town, the deer, opossum, and skunk.

The list would go on as he would say, "And Coyote found the wolf and collected its shit. And Coyote found the fly and collected its shit." I laughed when Coyote's list included tiny animals like flies and worms, animals so small I couldn't imagine what their feces would look like, much less conceive of Coyote collecting a tiny sample of something that was already so small it was invisible to the eye. On and on the list would grow as fish and birds were added, the list building through the force of its repetition in the same way that the Bible does. I didn't know it at the time, but he was using Coyote to tell me a creation story.

Once Coyote had collected a tiny bit of excrement from as many of the inhabitants of the earth as he could, he placed them all in a container. I can never remember what happens next. I don't know if Coyote was smoking or if lightning came out of the sky to strike this container that may or may not have been a trash can. What I do remember is that in some ironic way, Coyote's plan to destroy the earth with his atomic bomb was thwarted. When his bomb exploded too early, instead of destroying creation so that Coyote could rebuild the world from scratch, the earth was covered in a rain of everyone's shit. The result was that now everyone looked and smelled the same.

Rather than be disappointed, Coyote laughed and laughed, because he had, in fact, remade the world after all, but without having to destroy it. And thus, the atomic bomb turned out to be a tonic bomb that taught the highest, and the lowest, about humility, family, and respect for life.

I never talked about the Bible with my grandfather when I was a child. Because he had never learned to read or write, I assumed that he didn't know the stories I was learning about in catechism. I've always wondered what he would have thought about Job. I know he wouldn't have had any patience for Job's false friends. In his eyes, their false attempt to provide comfort would have made them *entremetidos*. My grandfather loathed nosey people who felt they had nothing better to do than buzz around a wound like flies. To him the Accuser would have been simply a good company man performing the task God gave him. And Job, I can hear my grandfather talking about how lucky Job was not just to have been given a second chance to serve faithfully but to be able to speak to God. If only we should all be so fortunate, he would have said.

I did ask him once why he never went to church. We were on the back porch sitting and staring at the quiet afternoon as usual. He flicked the ash from his cigarette, and then with the same hand, he motioned to the trees and the chickens, the garden, the meadows and the hills and the blank sky. "Dios no esta dentro de una iglesia. Dios esta aqui, mijo. Dios esta en el mundo."

I didn't know what to say, so I sat silently again.

I thought: Could God really have been all around me this whole time? Was he really in something as plain as a tree and not inside the buildings where we sang his praises? My grandfather would have delighted in Leviathan and Behemoth. I loved the idea of something so large and profound that your brain can't process it all at once, which means you can't measure it, or order it, you can just simply exist alongside it. The moving green of the mountains outside Seattle is like this for me. The Grand Canyon too.

By his neesings a light doth shine, and his eyes are like
the eyelids of the morning.
Out of his mouth go burning lamps, and sparks of fire
leap out.
Out of his nostrils goeth smoke, as out of a seething pot
or caldron.
His breath kindleth coals, and a flame goeth out of his
mouth.
In his neck remaineth strength, and sorrow is turned into
joy before him.

When I read these words from the book of Job, I can see my
grandfather's mouth again. His thin upper lip digs into the words
burning and *sparks*. The words kindle on his tongue. He never
learned to write or read, but yet he is. I can see the fire building
inside him until he reaches the word *joy* and pauses. He claps his
hand to the back of my neck and says, "before him." Joy is the
lesson his mouth teaches me. In his thick voice the words ring
true. I want to believe that God has planted the seeds of happiness
everywhere, even in the terrible jaws of Leviathan.

What greater proof of God's love could anyone need, other
than the monsters of the deep?

MY GRANDFATHER TAUGHT me we weren't supposed to cry.
This story is as old as men. And if not that old, then at least as
old as shame. Funerals were not an exception, he said. A funeral
is where a man would be most tested, in fact.

I turned this thought over, again and again.

I wanted to make him proud, make him see that I was just like
him. But how could I make sure I wouldn't be weak when I saw
someone I loved in a coffin? Just thinking of anyone from my
family dying was enough to make me feel overwhelmed, because I
could see their stiff face, feel the cold rail of the coffin against my

palm, smell the fresh pile of dirt to the side, could hear everyone's phlegm sucked into their throats. Then it hit me, I could use my imagination to practice for these dreaded moments.

And so I would wait until my parents left the house on an errand with my little brother. When I was sure I'd be alone for a couple of hours and everyone was safely gone, I would lie on my bed and think about how I would feel when someone I loved died. In no time flat, I was bawling like a baby. The long moans and tears came on in waves until my body shook and the muscles of my small stomach hurt. I would push past the point where I couldn't stand it anymore, until the grief had run its course.

I must have done this for years when I was a kid, slowly mourning my way through all the people I loved most in the world. I did this when I was fifteen for my friend Richard when we learned he had cancer and wouldn't live to see forty. Having already grieved him, I couldn't bring myself to attend his funeral. I already knew what he looked like and didn't see any point to visiting the body that no longer contained him. Richard never wore blush or powder. Who was the person in that perfumed body supposed to be?

I mourned both my grandparents in this way. My parents too.

When I was eight, I took care that there wouldn't be any sign of what I had been up to by the time my family returned to the house. I washed my face with a warm towel and then laid it over my eyes while I inhaled long and slow to try and steady my breathing. I didn't want puffed eyes or a runny nose to give me away.

At the end of it all, I was uplifted by the knowledge that the people I loved, and whose death I had just cried over, were still with me. Death never felt like an end. I never felt like anyone left me for good, unless I wanted them to. And that was as easy as not paying them any mind. And by "them," I don't mean their memory—I mean the person. I never needed a medium or a crystal ball to talk with the dead. My lips were good enough. I could speak with them any time I wanted and still enjoy their company. My dead were still living. That might seem strange or morbid to some, but the truth is that we're all walking dead when you stop and think about it.

After my aunt passed from cancer, my grandfather and I tended her grave on the weekends. We would weed not just her grave but also the shallow canals we had dug around the family plot, so that their crisscrossing would get water to the Bermuda grass that never wanted to take. After our work was done, we would sit awhile, not saying much of anything. I liked to imagine that in those moments, he was speaking to her in his mind, chatting about his life and how her daughter and boys were doing.

The last time I visited that cemetery, I noticed that the little canals my grandfather and I had dug were still there. Our tiny corner of the cemetery hadn't changed much; except, now my grandfather and grandmother were there. My uncle too.

My grandfather had said that one day it would fall on me to weed the plot just as he had shown me, to make sure that the canals were clear and that the grass was watered. I told him that I would, even though at the age of eleven I knew deep down that I wouldn't because when the time came, I would find a way to escape this town that felt like it was suffocating me. What's more, I knew that I wouldn't be losing my grandfather if I left, because he would not really be in that hole full of bones and dirt and rock.

It took me a long time before I broke my first promise to him. It wouldn't be long before I broke the next, and all the ones after that.

NOT YET. I can't let him go. It's been almost thirty years, and I can't let him go yet. Not now that I have made him laugh again in these pages.

See his leg. Watch it bounce with me. He has it folded over the other as he sits in his favorite chair on the porch.

The boy in my second-grade class who saw me during recess cross my legs in the same way said, "Why are you sitting like that? Don't you know only women and sissies sit like that?"

"How do you know?" I asked.

"Because my dad told me. Real men sit like this." He sat beside me and placed one ankle over his thigh.

"What's the difference?"

"My dad says crossing your legs like that is how women sit. When your legs are tight like that, it squishes your balls and makes you like a woman or like those guys who want to be like a woman. Real men need room to hang out."

My grandfather's leg bounces. I pretend to play with a toy so I can study him as he sits "like a woman."

His chest sags. A few long, wiry gray hairs surround his nipples. His belly is soft, and his legs are pale. Bald, he has a crown of thin silver hair. Faint scars of all different sizes mark his body like ghosts from the past. Even though I am just a boy, I want to be a man like him, the kind who doesn't let other people tell him what he is or isn't.

I never told my grandfather about the boy at school. If I had, he probably would have said something like the boy's father was a moron who wanted to look more manly because his wife's mustache was better than his own.

While he was a man of less-than-average height and weight, when I came near my grandfather, it was like standing beside a giant boulder that had sat in the sun all day. His presence was large, and he radiated confidence and love like heat.

While we hugged many times, I mostly remember the last one. His health had taken a sudden turn for the worse, and we had to admit him to the hospital. Even though he was eighty-six and had emphysema and one of his lungs had long since shriveled and turned the color of a prune, he had seemed indestructible.

After the funeral, my grandmother told me that black magic had killed my grandfather. A witch in Mexico had placed a clumsy death hex on someone else and it had gone astray. My grandmother said she had dealt with the witch and that her incompetence would never hurt another person again.

I wish I knew what I whispered in his ear the last time I saw him.

I know I wept.

I know I kissed his cheek.

Then, like all disappointed children, I tried to punish the world a thousand times over for being itself.

Symmetry

Comfy socks. Phone near where I'll sit. A glass of water. My apartment is still.

When I choose one of the twenty-five books I'm currently reading, I think, *What a weirdo*, and then: Yes, but a weirdo who is also the counter of lines, the marker of beginnings and endings, an oldest son and a middle child, whose nose is allergic to the air and the trees in all seasons, the devourer of apples and the hater of peaches, a bastard who was given three chances at a father, the enemy of tomatoes and raw fish and milk, the stomach grumbling behind you, the patron of cats both feral and not, the disciple of the tigress that suckles the orphaned piglet.

A few slight adjustments and the parallel lines that my books, shoes, phone, couch, and pillows send out away from themselves are in harmony with the lines of the windows, counter, walls, floor, and doors. I am a spider in the center of a perfect web. I am hungry, always hungry, but I do not know for what.

I put my feet on the ottoman and open Kafka's *The Blue Octavo Notebooks*. My cat stretches her black arm with the white glove on the end of it across my stomach. Her other arm also looks like it has a white glove. Her name is Lindsey, and she is black with white, and it looks like she's wearing orange shorts with high white socks. Cat books call her a tortoiseshell, although just like other cats that look like her, she does not resemble a tortoise. Or a turtle, for that matter. Like a tortoise, she is feisty and will snap at you if you place your hand in front of her face. Though, I suppose anything would.

For two years, starting in 1917, instead of writing in his usual diaries, Kafka took to writing in octavo-sized notebooks. He filled eight of these smaller notebooks with parts of stories, as well as his thoughts on the hope and suffering we encounter between our birth and death. Until I jump to another book, my mind is at rest. No counting, just drinking the words someone poured onto a page.

I am tired. So tired.

The pages of the book are dark, because the book is in my right hand and its cover faces away from the dark kitchen toward the window. When I grow tired and switch hands, the sunlight from the window makes the words sharper.

Lindsey looks at me and blinks slowly. I've read that when one cat does this to another, it means, "I love you." What can it mean for me? And if a blink of an eye can mean a whole sentence, what have I been saying to the world all my life?

It would be years before Lindsey learned to accept love as easily as she gave it. I'm not even afraid to pet her when she sleeps beside me anymore, even though she is nearly invisible in the dark. Her previous owner said Lindsey had had two kittens when she was young. One was given away, and the other was kept. Her son, named Tiger, and Oscar, another cat they lived with, bullied her at mealtime. Even after she had enough and left, Oscar came around to fight with her. He didn't know she had a family now, that she was no longer just a cat named after the street she lived on but Lindsey Anne Lou Sticktail Morín.

She hovers near my desk while I type this. I check the clock. It's 4:23 p.m. She likes to eat dinner at 4:30 p.m.

Like me, she dislikes daylight savings, because it throws our routines off. I ask her to wait, and I keep typing. She climbs the stairs to the couch and heads toward my desk.

I click Save As . . .

I grab her wet food from the refrigerator.

Four seconds in the microwave and stir.

Arthritis doesn't keep her from trotting after me. I tap the white ceramic bowl that has always been her dinner bell. I'm positive she's been deaf for over a year, and yet I can't help but ring it, just in case. She gobbles her food as if it is the last time she will ever eat. Once she has finished, I wipe her runny nose, rinse the bowl, and return here.

She is purring because she was hungry and now she is not.

This year she turned nineteen. I met her when she was three or four and walked up to me in a parking lot. While she was rubbing my legs, I stroked her back. She wheeled and tried to scratch me. Surprised, I watched her run off. We repeated this scene the next few months before she tried moving into our apartment. Since she and our cat didn't get along, we tried everything to keep her out. We shook plastic bags to scare her and even sprayed her with water. Nothing worked. A few months later, when she scratched her owner for trying to carry her home, we knew then she had chosen us, had marked the moment in blood, and was ours.

Though the sun is low, what little is left of it still makes it easier to see now the shapes of the letters Kafka strung together to write, "One can disintegrate the world by means of very strong light. For weak eyes the world becomes solid, for still weaker eyes it seems to develop fists, for eyes weaker still it becomes shamefaced and smashes anyone who dares to gaze upon it."

The world demands to be seen, gets angry when it isn't. When the moon is out tonight, it won't matter which hand I hold my book in. The darkness of my kitchen will be the same as the darkness outside. The only difference will be that I know where all the sharp objects sleep in one. As for the other, who can say?

Shamefaced

I love thee with a love I seemed to lose
With my lost saints.

My lips should be the color of figs.

Around the edges, the soft purple tint still remains. My lips were the same color as my father's until I entered the sixth grade. This was around the time when my mom told him to leave and not come back. It was also when I started to walk around with the collar of my shirts in my mouth.

Did I love the salty taste of my sweat my collars would collect? Sure. But I also hated the way the wet material would feel against my chest when I dropped it from my mouth. Why did I do something that would have drawn attention to me, that would have made me run the risk of being seen as a weirdo?

Because it felt good. It felt good to hide a third of my face in my shirt. If my collar was in my mouth, then no one would know whether I was smiling or frowning. With my father gone, I didn't know how to be anymore. His leaving left me with questions I didn't know how to answer.

Should I still keep an eye out for the police?

Was it safe to invite friends over now?

Did people know he had gone back to his family?

When would I see him?

Did I still have to sleep lightly in case I was needed in the middle of the night?

Was I still his son?

Did he still love me?

Love us?

I didn't know the answer to any of those questions that circled in my mind over and over. What I did know was that I felt calm with part of me hidden under the tent of my shirt. Sometimes I would even pull my arms inside my shirt so that I was even more hidden. And what I know now is that the salt on my collars dried out my lips.

Once my lips were dry, they broke, and in breaking, bits of them lifted and curled. Those tiny bits of skin were like brail on my lips. At first, I just ran my tongue against them over and over. One day, I pulled my upper lip in and rubbed it against my teeth. My eye watered as the thin strip of skin I had just peeled away hung down from my lip. I had pulled it away so fast and easy, I felt the pain after the fact.

There was nothing left to do but pull it off.

It was so thin I could barely feel it between my fingers. I thought pulling it fast and hard would hurt less.

I was wrong.

Instead of breaking right off, the strip of skin pulled farther up my lip and bled. After I wiped away more tears, I twisted the skin gently between my fingers until it broke off at the base.

As the months passed and I kept sucking on my shirt collars, I continued to pull the skin from my lips. Before long, it became a game to see how long I could make a strip of skin before it reached the edge of my lip. When one lip would become sore and needed time to heal from the damage, I would let it rest by peeling the skin from the other lip.

Peel

Bleed

Twist

Repeat

For some reason, no one seemed to say anything about my collar chewing or the awful state of my lips. Before long, I discovered scabs.

The first time I squeezed the pimples on my arms dry and there was nothing left but blood, I thought that would be the end of it. By the next day, rough disks covered the small spots on my arm I had messed with. When the scabs were hard enough, I peeled them off slowly.

I stared at the little circle of dried blood on the tip of my finger. My body had somehow magically made it overnight. I marveled at how something so perfect and simple could have come from me. The next day, it was back, only a little bigger. For a while, I entertained myself by trying to make the scabs as big as possible by pulling them off at just the right times. Because they were hidden under my shirtsleeves, and sometimes my arms were inside my shirt, no one noticed the constellations of scars I was building on my upper arms.

By the middle of that school year, sucking my shirt collars and peeling my scabs stopped making me feel better. Without the salt from my collars to dry out my lips, they stopped peeling. When my lips healed, their purple had been replaced with the pale pink of a grapefruit wedge when you hold it up to the light.

My new obsession was spitting. I had seen my father spit all my life. When I launched a thin stream of spit eight feet away, the guys in my grade were impressed. One of them even called me Scupetín whenever he would see me. I thought to myself,

This is it—this will be the nickname by which everyone in Mathis will know me. I would be Scupetín, the son of El Indio. I imagined that wherever I would go, people would greet me with a smile because my name was fun to say.

My nickname never caught on. After a month, even the guy who thought up the name stopped calling me that. Nothing had changed. I was still as invisible as I had been before I had quietly mutilated my lips and arms.

My father was gone.

For good this time.

While my mouth was now a lighter color and no longer a small replica of his, I felt connected to my father every time I spit. He was the man, and I was the shadow.

Every day for the next fifteen years, I spit on the ground without apology. Then the day came when I saw a young man do it. Shame rushed warm through my body, and I stopped. For 5,475 days, I had been my father's son. And then I wasn't. And I let him go.

I TOLD MY baby brother all about the Greeks and their Hades. You could live down there and not just float on lakes of fire like the Catholic church taught us.

The high school librarian ordered all the books on Greek mythology that I had asked for. She could tell I was hungry for new stories.

Before the Greeks, I read about Davy Crockett and Jim Bowie. I told my brother about the trappers and explorers, and so my baby brother walked around the house in red shorts and a tank top carrying my Bowie knife. Its blade was ten inches long. He put it in his boot that used to be my boot.

He moved across our patch of world like fire. He was forever running, even when he wasn't moving. When he slept, he sweat. He was a delightful flame that burned because it could.

More and more knives appeared in time. They were under his pillow, between the cushions of the sofa, knives in all the dark places I couldn't see, knives Jim Bowie and I had never heard of in all shapes and sizes. After his friends multiplied shiny and bright, I moved on to tell him stories about the big wars that set country against country.

He squatted, one leg out, the other bent, something long and thin on his shoulder. He aimed his imaginary bazooka at my mom's boyfriend Toro. He aimed it at the heart that sent blood to the fists.

Was it a broom my brother was holding? Or an umbrella whose sights he slowly adjusted, balanced on his shoulder, as his clear eye squinted true just before the whoosh that knocked him to the floor with a laugh. But it never rained in our part of Texas, so how could it be an umbrella? "Maybe it was your mind you were holding," I want to tell him.

When his third-grade teacher put duct tape on his mouth and sat him in front of the class for talking, this is a story we hadn't read before. When she wasn't looking, he poked a hole with a pencil so he could breathe. It was not enough, because his fire went out that day.

"Why do you think so much? You always have to analyze everything?" my brother, now a man, once said to me.

My silence tells him, *I don't know*, when what I want to say is, *If someone doesn't analyze our lives, then how will we ever know we didn't deserve the life we had?*

You're the man of the house now.

These were my father's words after he moved out. When my grandfather echoed them a week later, I assumed it was true. I was excited about my new role. Besides, *take care of your mother and little brother* sounded easy enough.

Less than a year later came the night I woke to my mom sobbing in her bedroom on the other side of the wall. Toro was the first man my mom dated after she kicked my father out of the house. While I listened and tried to decide whether to check on her, I heard her new boyfriend yell, "Shut the fuck up!"

Then I heard a bird slam into a window.

In all their years together, my father had never hit my mom. I then heard more crying, as bird after bird slammed against a window I couldn't see.

I was paralyzed by fear. My mom entered my bedroom and sat on the edge of my bed while I prayed for the injured birds I knew didn't exist. I cracked my eyes to a tiny slit to see if my little brother was still asleep in the bed across from mine. Toro had been nothing but nice since my mom had met him at the Monte Carlo bar. He was about as tall as my father, but where my father was lean, Toro was like a barrel made of muscle. He walked with his chest out as if he had something to prove.

I could feel him standing in the doorway. His steps grew heavier as he walked closer. He was by my bed now. He was panting like someone who had just finished a game of basketball. I could smell his nakedness. His sweat was an ugly hand in the dark.

"Come to bed, baby. You know I didn't mean it."

"Go away."

I waited for the sound of footsteps to signal he had left the room, but there was only a long silence, at the end of which I heard, "Touch it."

"No."

"Come on, touch it."

"No. Get out of here before the boys wake up."

"You'll be sorry," he said, as he walked away.

In the morning, my mom's face looked like an apple that had once rolled off the kitchen table. Because I was hungry and it was all we had, I took it to school anyway. I polished it on my shirt and ate its brown, mealy bruises with shame. The next few months that followed were like a whirlpool that tossed us between calm and violence.

TORO SWUNG THE chain to whip us, as we moved in the moonlight around and around our van.

If you had seen us from the street, you might have thought we were playing a family game. We were. It was called hide-and-seek. We won when we woke up in a motel parking lot and saw him drive by without seeing us.

HIS HEAVY WALK from the living room to the kitchen stopped in the middle of the hall. I looked up just as the light caught Toro's eye.

He was watching me through the crack between the restroom door and the wall. I pretended to read my comic book and waited for him to leave. When my mom shuffled dishes in the sink, his eye disappeared and I heard him walk away. When I finished and washed my hands, I stuffed a washcloth in the crack, but it fell out, because it wasn't thick enough. I tried a hand towel, but it was too short. Toro might stoop and look into the bathroom when I was in there. Finally, I tried one of the bath towels I had used as a cape when I was younger. It was thick enough and long enough. While I wouldn't be able to fly out of our house anymore, at least now no one could look into the bathroom.

OUR GRAN TORINO flew toward 120 miles per hour.

The more we screamed, the more Toro laughed.

The car rose from the asphalt like a white missile with blue stripes. Everything could end any second. We could hit a bump and land in a field of corn, ready to explode. Or we could hit the red brick walls of the carwash and bloom into a thousand roses on the concrete. In the morning, someone would come along and power wash us away.

I LEFT MY bed and sleepwalked to the living room, where Toro stood over my mom. He had thrown her on the couch and now his hands were at her throat.

She was almost gone.

In a second, she would slip into the peaceful black from where she would no longer call me with her mind, in a voice I couldn't hear, because there was no sound. Except, there I was, asleep, placing my little hand softly on his sweaty, straining shoulder that was ending her life until he saw me, let go, and stumbled out the door into the wordless night.

MY MOTHER SAID the Monte Carlo was packed when she saw Toro across the room, sitting among friends with his back to her. They had been broken up for a few weeks after he beat her for the better part of a year. Before she met Toro, my mom had never been a drinker.

She walked up behind him and whispered in his ear, "Don't ever bother me or my family again." The New Year was only hours away as she stumbled away to cry in the parking lot.

When Toro grabbed her shoulder in the parking lot and said, "Baby," she wheeled around, her hands like a Weed Eater. Over and over, she yelled, "Leave me alone!" He cried out and stumbled back, while she climbed in her friend's car and drove away.

MONTHS LATER, just before my twelfth birthday, I thought it was time to tell my mom during a party at our house that I had heard her all those nights she had begged for help on the other side of my bedroom wall, begged for mercy from Toro's fists that fell and fell.

My guilt had made me heavy. Around my mom I seemed to move slower, every step a struggle. I had wondered: Is this my punishment for not helping her? Was my curse to grow into a human sack of sand? Unless I did something, I feared that one day she would check on me after I didn't get up for school and find me in bed transformed into a stuffed toy with a broken string that couldn't talk anymore.

I watched her laugh and let loose. This was the first time I had ever seen her drink. She seemed freer than she had been in years. I started to talk to her, but the music was so loud she couldn't hear me so I asked her onto the porch.

"Mom, there's something I've been wanting to tell you."

"What is it, mijo?"

I had never heard music so loud in our house before. I looked over her shoulder through our front door at her friends dancing inside. I couldn't remember ever seeing anyone dance in our living room. In any room in our house, for that matter. I thought that after a few minutes of conversation, maybe some crying as we hugged, she would go back inside and talk with her friends and I would feel better.

"You know how sometimes Toro would . . ."

"Berta, you want another beer?" one of her friends said. My mom turned to her friend and said, "In a minute. I'm talking with my son right now. I'll get one when I go inside."

"You know how . . . Mom, do you remember when Toro would hit you at night when we were asleep?"

"Yeah, what about it, mijo?"

I could tell she didn't know what I was going to say next by the way her face looked like a cloud drifting across the surface of a pool.

"A lot of those nights, I could hear Toro hitting you. I could hear you asking him to stop. And I didn't do anything to help you. I'm so sorry."

She tried to slap me, but I moved out of the way. "Why didn't you help me? I needed you," she repeated, as she lunged toward me and tried to grab my hair.

The friend who had asked her about a drink had come back and wrapped my mom in her arms and said, "She doesn't mean it, mijo. Go. I'll take care of her."

On that night, the last night she would ever touch alcohol, my gentle, kind mom had tried to hurt me. When my brother and I were younger and we were supposed to be hit with the belt because we had misbehaved, she would always leave it to my father to do. She would lock herself in her bedroom and cover her ears, because she couldn't bear to hear my brother or me cry.

I walked across the street to my friend Jackie's in a daze. Despite his advice, my failure as the man of the house grew in my mind like a glacier. For fifteen years, it sat solid, giving nothing of itself, and then one day, it cracked when I confronted her about what she had said. To my shock, she didn't remember anything about that night.

In my mother's memory, my confession had never happened. All the guilt I felt for not helping her when she was being abused, for making her so angry with me, seemed wasted.

As we sat across from each other in the living room like strangers, all she could say was, "But you saved me, you saved me . . ." as she wept, and then her heart did what it did best and blew out of her like a hot wind with nowhere to go.

I MISSED CLASS the day they taught the tricks of courting: aloofness, patience, gifts, timing, presentation? The list seemed endless, and I had no clue where to start. When I learned that Rhonda liked me back, as any shy eighth-grade kid would do, I searched for her in the halls between classes, my heart thumping, in the hope of exchanging goofy smiles.

Rhonda was a seventh grader with long, curly brown hair who had the cool slouch of a smoker when she stood with her friends, even though there wasn't a cigarette in sight. When my friends had caught me staring in the direction of a couple of girls, they asked if I liked one of them.

"Yeah. I think so."

"Which one?"

"The curly hair one."

"They both have curly hair."

"The one with the jean jacket."

"We can go ask her if she likes you. Do you want us to?"

"I don't know."

Sweat dripped from my palms to the ground. What if they went over and she said she liked me too? Or worse, what if she said she didn't? I'd be humiliated. Even though it only took me a few seconds to think about it, with my friends egging me on to be brave, I said yes.

Just the year before, when I was newly arrived to junior high as a seventh grader, one of the cool eighth-grade girls had flirted with me in gym class. Her name was Molly. She had short black hair, biceps big enough to intimidate any seventh-grade boy or girl, and a voice that sounded like the bottom of a pie tin when you run your fork along it. She teased me in the gym while the class did laps around the basketball court by walking close enough behind me so that when my arm swung back, my hand would land against her crotch.

After that, I think I sent her a note saying I liked her. When she said she liked me, too, my mind raced in a way it had never done before. She was bold and didn't care what anyone thought, unlike the other girls I knew.

On the walk home, I sang "When a Man Loves a Woman" until my throat hurt. Even though we never really hung out, much less went on anything resembling a date, I was heartbroken when she said her family was about to move from Mathis. When school was empty, on a wooden pole where people ate lunch outside, as high as I could reach, I mustered the courage to carve a heart with our initials inside it.

Thinking about Molly, I became less nervous as my friends walked over to talk to Rhonda. For all I knew, she would be as excited about me liking her as I had been about Molly liking me. When they came back, they said that she liked me a lot.

For a few days, I said hi every time I saw her in the hall. When I tried to talk to her at lunch, she moved away with a worried look on her face. When my friends thought I had made enough of a fool of myself, they finally told me the truth. She didn't like me.

For a week, I was angry and embarrassed and didn't know what to do. After a few days passed, I finally had what seemed like a great plan to restore my reputation. I couldn't let myself be known as the loser that was so gullible that he believed a beautiful girl could like an ugly guy like him back.

For my idea to work, I needed the courtyard to be packed with my classmates milling around before the lunch period ended. I also needed someone who was crazy enough to believe the lie I had in mind. Once I had steered the conversation with a guy named Jimmy toward comic books, the day felt right to set things straight. As Jimmy talked about his favorite characters, I looked around at all the skaters, shitkickers, jocks, nerds, and populars hovering around their own little groups. It was time. If I was lucky, then my rumor would spread quickly.

"Have you ever heard of Wolverine?" I asked Jimmy.

"Yeah, the guy with the claws."

"It's not just claws. That metal his claws are made out of, it's in his whole body. On his bones."

"Wow."

"Yeah, makes him pretty indestructible."

"That's pretty cool."

"He's my favorite character."

"Because of the claws?"

"Nah, cause I'm just like him. My bones are laced with metal too."

"Get the fuck out of here. You're so full of shit!"

"It's true. A couple summers back, I was helping my father work on his truck. I was underneath it when the jack slipped, and it fell on me."

"Holy shit. Is that true?"

"It broke almost every bone in my body."

"Fuck."

"The only thing the doctors could do was reinforce all my bones with steel."

"You're so full of shit. Prove it."

"Alright. How much do you think I weigh?"

"I don't know. Maybe 110?"

"That's pretty close. Try and pick me up, and you'll see I feel a lot heavier. Like 150 or something."

Jimmy hugged me and tried to lift me. "You're right. How come?"

"It's cause of the steel, man." Even though I was a skinny kid, a bully who tried to pick me up had said I was heavier than I looked. I thought using this fact would be all the proof I needed.

"I don't know. Through your whole body? That sounds made up. Let me test it."

"Okay, but how?"

"Stand here in front of the metal door and let me ram my shoulder into your chest. But first I'll need a running start. If your bones are laced with steel, then it won't hurt you, right?"

Jimmy's smile at the end of his question made me wonder if I had picked the right guy. Since he had been held back a grade, Jimmy was bigger and stronger than most of us. He even looked like he had started shaving already. I wondered what Jimmy smashing my chest with his shoulder at full speed would do to me. There was a crowd of people listening to us. If I backed down now, then I would look like even more of a fool.

"You're right. It won't hurt me at all."

"Are you sure?" Jimmy asked, as he started backing up for his running start.

"If that's what it'll take for you to believe me." More people were watching now. I half hoped that Rhonda was too.

"Okay. Stand right there in front of the door. You can't be chickenshit and move, or else I'll hit the door and hurt myself."

"Why would I move when there's no chance I'm going to get hurt?"

"Alright. One, two, three . . ." Jimmy sprinted the twenty feet and struck my chest like a sledgehammer. I felt my back slam against the door, right before I bent over and put my hands on my knees trying to catch my breath.

"Are you okay? I thought you were going to move for sure."

"I'm good. Just knocked the air out of me. I didn't say my lungs had steel. Just my bones."

"Wow. I guess you were really telling the truth."

When I forced myself to stand straight in spite of the dull pain that was spreading, I couldn't resist asking him how his shoulder was and expressing how worried I had been that he might break it against the metal plate in my chest. If he had any doubts left, my concern for him clinched the lie. By the end of the week, people had heard the rumor about my steel bones.

In a few days, I went from being the boy I thought everyone saw as a loser who had been tricked into believing a girl liked him to a freak of modern medicine and science.

When I felt the lie had firmly replaced my embarrassment over Rhonda, I casually confessed to a friend that I had made the whole thing up. After some work convincing a few people that my bones were not in fact laced with steel, people looked at me with a blend of surprise and disappointment. My classmates couldn't quite decide whether I was a liar, a clown, or both. To me their confusion meant they didn't know how to categorize me. I was happy to be invisible again, no different than the pole in the yard on which people carved the anarchist *A*, curse words, and hearts with initials in them when they thought no one was looking.

I THOUGHT I KNEW all about prayer. To really beg something or someone you can't see for help. Toro taught me what it really meant to pray. I still remember when God didn't stop him from beating my mom again—I began to pray to all the saints my grandmother kept statues of. When St. Lazarus and Mary and Michael and the other angels didn't help, I gave up on them all.

How many nights I stared out my window when the house was quiet and everyone was asleep. I was looking for something in those stars, an answer to our troubles in some pattern I couldn't see. Hadn't the stars guided people for thousands of years? I never could find the shapes the Greeks saw up there. Except for one of the dippers. The small one, I think.

One night, I saw a shooting star. Knowing what every kid knows, I closed my eyes and wished. I forgot to count how many days passed before the next beating. It wasn't many, I'm sure.

Sometimes the quiet days were harder. What can you do with all that peace and quiet when you know the hammer will fall again at any moment and your mom will still be under it?

Later a teacher told my class that most of the stars were the light of suns millions of years away that had already died. I knew then why the shooting star hadn't worked. Why no answer ever came from the heavens. It was all death up there. I don't know what my classmates thought of all that. For me, it all suddenly made sense.

I stopped looking up at the night for the most part after that. What was the point of looking at all that dead light? I was through wasting my time on what didn't have any power. If I wanted to see death, I didn't need to look up to find it. When I was a kid, Death sat across the kitchen table from me every day in Toro's jeans and T-shirts with the sleeves cut off.

There would be no heroes coming from the night sky. There weren't any coming from earth, either. Not my grandfather, who was too old, or my father or Jackie or any of the other neighbors, who didn't see what was happening in our home as any of their business.

Years after my mom split with Toro, word came to Mathis that he had died. People said some new girlfriend he had been beating had hit him in the head with a baseball bat. He lay in a coma for a few days, and then he was gone.

I wonder if, after the bat touched him, he had enough time to pray. And if he did, whom he prayed to. If only he had ever wanted to talk to me when he was dating my mom, I could have told him not to waste his time with prayer.

A few years ago when a friend started talking about how beautiful the stars looked, I shrugged. There are no heroes coming from the sky to save anybody. If people barely care enough to help each other out, there's no way any salvation is coming down from all that black peppered with dead light.

On Intrusive Thoughts

It first happened in my apartment. Lindsey was purring on the couch when my mind became a screen where someone had dimmed the lights and what I saw was in 3D high-definition IMAX in the way dreams are, only I wasn't asleep. I had tried that, going to sleep I mean, tried to go to sleep so I could stop having this waking dream, no, it was a nightmare, a waking nightmare, and if I told you that what I saw was only two seconds long, you would be forgiven for thinking that this was a blessing, only you would be wrong, because if you were strapped to your chair so that you couldn't walk out, the movie on the screen could be shown, and restarted, hundreds of times on one endless loop, which is the exact opposite of a blessing, but your eyes, turn your head and close your eyes, *that's what I would do*, you think, and you would not be wrong for expecting that to work, after all, how many times have we looked away from what we couldn't bear and felt a momentary relief, only whoever was the projectionist thought of this, too, because when I shut my eyes, the inside of my eyelids became the screen, a screen on which I saw my bedroom door five feet away from me, ajar, and at the foot of that door was my sweet Lindsey, just her head, peeking in, looking for me, just before the door slammed shut on it, on her, and the crunch of bone I heard was the sound you make when you bite an apple, and peek, slam, crunch continued on loop for hours every day and everywhere: my office, at the grocery store, the gym, the car, and because I couldn't escape it, I told my therapist I tried to engage the nightmare with some other part of my mind, the part that gave me absolute control of my dreams in which it was not unusual for me to pause a car about to hit me and then move it with a swipe of my hand, that part of my mind let me enter, let me stop only bearing witness, so that I put my hand on that stubborn door in order to stop the violence my heart couldn't bear, and then it happened, the door slammed, chopped off my fingers, and I tell you, I never tried that again, never tried to resist, just learned to smile through it all as I walked through life as a secret horror show, and I shouldn't say much more, even though I talked about this for months with my trauma counselor, who said this was an escalation of my OCD, and my reluctance, my reluctance is not what you think, it's that I'm scared that I might have already said too much, gone on for too long, and in so doing woken up the projectionist in my head who hasn't run this movie, or any movie for that matter, in almost two years now, no, it's better to leave him sleeping in that projector room of my mind where, I like to think, he is asleep in the pajamas I wore when I was eleven because he is me at that age, the age when I often fell asleep in front of the TV that had long since turned to snow.

Childhood's Faith

I love thee with the passion put to use
In my old griefs, and with my childhood's faith.

I was lucky to have fathers.

One two three.

Left Right Left.

Jackie Eugene Powell was born in Austin in 1955. He was the father of two sons he didn't see as often as he wished he did. His eyes were the color of melted caramel. His hair was just two shades darker than that, and he wore it in either an afro or cut close to his scalp.

He worked off the books as a plumber, carpenter, security guard, mechanic, roofer, landscaper, house sitter, and driver and, most frequently, with a mobile home company transporting and setting up single and double-wides. He once told me he founded and ran a successful commercial carpet-cleaning company in Austin, a business he was squeezed out of by one of his partners, a man in a wheelchair. That taught him, he said, "even cripples can be crooks."

Jackie and I were lucky. We gave each other a second chance, for me to be the good son and for him to be the good father, roles we weren't very good at playing with our own flesh and blood. I wouldn't know until much later that the family I found would mean as much to me as the family I inherited.

After my father was gone, Jackie and I were drawn to each other like magnets. I had no dad now, and he missed his son who was the same age I was, a son he said he couldn't see because of his inability to get clean. Since I had grown up around drugs all my life, there was no problem if Jackie was high around me or, later, when I could drive and had a car, if I took him to score. Around me, he was free to do what he wanted.

Jackie lived catty-corner from the house where I grew up in Mathis. If you passed my house and crossed the street, there was Jackie's place at the end of the block, a block whose street dead-ended at the tracks that ran behind his house. Trees and bushes made it hard to see the front of the house if you drove by. If you walked up to the front door, it wouldn't have helped any, because you couldn't get through the small, overgrown yard. And even if you did make it to the front door, no one could answer if you knocked, because it was boarded up from the inside.

It'd probably been years before anyone had gone in or out of that door. If you went in through the back door, you'd walk into Jackie's bedroom, the only room he used in a house that had no water, electricity, or heat. He cooked outside over a fire, and when he needed to use the restroom, there was an outhouse snuggled deep in the tall weeds.

He hadn't always lived this way.

Jackie was raised in that house by his Aunt Beulah. If I close my eyes, time flickers, and a young Jackie springs off that porch into the night to catch a ride to the high school football game, a game in which he would be a star, one of the town heroes. He is younger but just as fit as when I knew him as a grown man. Only, when he was a kid, the lack of fat on his five-foot-ten frame was from All-District, and sometimes All-State, seasons in basketball, football, track, and baseball, as opposed to the way crack and cocaine would keep his metabolism revved up.

"Aunt Beulah was hard on me."

"What do you mean, Jack?"

"If I misbehaved, she'd tell me to get a switch from outside. If I got one that was too flimsy, she'd beat me until it broke and then make me go outside and get a good one and then beat me until that one broke. I'd spend the rest of the day pulling wood out of my skin. She was old school and didn't fuck around."

Over the years, he would tell me how much he loved Aunt Beulah, even if she made him feel unwanted. After a few years, I found the courage to ask him why his aunt raised him. He didn't know why his mother didn't want him, only that she didn't was his response. Aunt Beulah was his momma, and he loved her. And that was that.

Some of his relatives told me he had been given away because he had been too hard to handle as a child. Others said it was because his father was unstable and wouldn't leave his mother alone. Eventually, he shared with me stories about his sisters and brother, describing them in detail, what they had in common and what they didn't. He told me his mother loved shar-peis. When he told me that he never stopped missing her, the iceberg I always sensed when he talked about his family cracked. Inside of him something broke. His eyes wet, he stared into the distance. His silence had the heaviness of ice. I sensed something inside him slide into the cold waters of disillusionment.

IT HAPPENED DURING my second year of high school.

It was the middle of the week.

It was after school, because I wore pants and my shirt was untucked.

Sometimes I remember being alone, and at other times, my cousin Anthony is beside me. I am in the parking lot of H-E-B, the local grocery store.

I've parked in such a way that my truck faces away from the store.

It was spring, because the afternoon was sharp with summer light.

The dull light of fall in South Texas never predicts anything but its own end.

I see my father.

He walks out of the store as I approach. He has not lived with us for six years.

I smile.

I walk faster.

He passes a Coke machine, a Pepsi machine, and a machine containing all the sodas of H-E-B.

Sometimes I remember him being alone, and at other times he is with his wife.

"Hey, Dad."

"Hi, mijo."

Before I can lean in for a kiss, he extends his arm to shake my hand.

My hand is weak.

His grip is firm and mechanical.

His hand is as hard as any of the thousands of bricks he laid in his life.

He hugs me awkwardly.

When we say goodbye, he looks as confused as I do.

The inside of the store is a fog.

That was the last time my father broke my heart. Greeting him with a kiss on his cheek had been as natural for us as shaking hands is for other fathers and sons. A slap to the face would have left me less embarrassed than his hand reaching out.

Maybe he did not want to be embarrassed in front of his wife or to make her embarrassed. The next time I saw him, he did not reach his hand to me. His lips on my cheek were warm.

He taught me love sometimes doesn't vanish completely like in the movies. There are times when it is big enough that it can only die one piece at a time.

He had been trying to teach me this my whole life.

It took the bittersweet light of spring for me to see it.

SO MY FATHER only wanted to shake my hand now. What did I care? I could live with that. Besides, Jackie still hugged me. He even mussed my hair or hung an arm around my shoulder when he wanted to comfort me or when he felt proud. Sometimes, when we were out of town on an errand or to score him some dope, people who didn't know us would call me his son, and we would smile and not correct them.

When we were around people Jackie had grown up with in Mathis, I realized that the last thing some people wanted was for him to touch them. Jackie was poor, and his house had no electricity or running water. Sometimes, he only bathed once every two weeks at my house or with a bar of soap under the water hose next door.

Once, while he worked an odd job for some mechanics he considered friends, they joked when he was out of earshot, not realizing I spoke Spanish, about how his body odor grew ten-fold when he had lifted his leg to put a foot on a car bumper. I thought they were kidding. I had known Jackie for years and spent time with him almost every day and never noticed what they described.

I stared past them at the yellow grass in the field across the street as one of the men flicked his head in my direction and said to his friends, "¿Entiende español?"

"¿Quién sabe?" one of them said with a shrug.

The muscles along my ribs quivered as my stomach tightened into the fist I wanted to hit them with. I had never punched a man before. Standing before these men who were about the same age as my father, I shook inside. For all the adrenaline pumping through me, I couldn't muster the courage to say, "Yes, I understand Spanish," and shame them for talking about Jackie, a man I was proud people mistook for my father.

A second later, Jackie walked out from behind the garage with a grin. He announced we were going to the store for more beer, and we left. As we drove away, he asked me what was wrong.

"They were talking about you in Spanish, Jack. They thought I didn't understand, and I didn't say anything. They said . . ."

"Stop, grasshopper. I don't need to know what those fat fucks said. Do you think anything they say about me matters?"

"I'm sorry. I . . ."

"Listen. What have I always told you? Never let them see you sweat. That means no one. Those motherfuckers can only protect themselves against what they know. Now that they think you don't speak Spanish, you can be my ears when I'm not around. If they say something important like how they're going to cheat old Jack, then you can warn me. What do you say?"

"Are you sure?"

"Look at this smile? Does it look like I'm mad?"

As he disappeared into the store, the heat danced in waves across the empty parking lot. It was triple digits all week. When a stiff wind blew into my truck, I drew a long breath until the smell of Jackie's body clung from my nose to the back of my throat. If I poured pepper in your nose and then dunked your head in a river, I guess you could say it smelled like that. A little like joy. A little like life.

JACKIE WAS WOUND like a ball of rubber bands. His left leg twitched, and then it went still. On the table between us were a piece of cotton and a needle. He never cared much for snorting coke, though he would if he were in a rush. I studied his face in the same way he now studied something outside his house.

"Did you hear that?"

"Hear what, Jack?"

He lifted his hand, folded all his fingers except his index and thumb and said, "There. You hear it?"

"No."

"Come here. Sit right here and look with me. Through the window about twenty feet past the yard in the bushes. You see?"

"By the outhouse?"

"To the left. Do you see something moving?"

He had stopped blinking, and his lips stuck out a little in the way yours might if you were about to kiss your mother on the cheek. Sweat had begun to drip down his head. Now my leg bounced, and I thought about my father and how if it weren't for all my time spent as a child around him while he was high, I wouldn't be able to sit with this man I loved as he, too, became lost in another world.

"I don't see anything, Jack. I think it's just the wind moving the weeds."

"Are you sure?"

"Yeah, it's just the wind. That's all. Or maybe a cat."

"Okay, Mas. I trust you."

His leg twitched again, and he blinked. I hung my head and stared at the floor of his room. Through a small hole between my feet, I counted all the things that had fallen and gotten trapped between the floorboards. I looked up and started counting the seconds between each time he blinked. I almost reached thirty once. Then the twitching in his leg slowed down, and he closed his eyes and took a deep breath.

"I see the wind now. Thanks, bro. Thanks for not leaving me. And for sitting with me while I was tweaking. I could never do this with my sons, you know? But I don't have to hide from you. You can see I'm no good, and you stay anyway."

"There's nothing wrong with you, Jack."

"You wanna know how I know you got a good heart?"

"How?"

"Because I know you believe that. Even if it isn't true. A lot of good people have given up on old Jack. And they were right to. I'm nobody. And when I'm gone, no one's gonna remember me except for maybe you. And I hope you don't think about me too much, because you have your life to live. I don't wanna get in the way of it, especially after I'm gone."

I hated it when he ran himself down like this, especially when he saw himself as something worthless that just needed to pass out of the world.

"Will you promise me something, Mas?"

"Sure, Jack. What is it?"

"If you ever become a writer, write about all of this. Don't leave anything out, okay?"

"What makes you think I would be a writer?"

"Those poems you wrote for school were good. I'm just saying, if you do, don't leave anything out. I want people to know what a fucked-up place Mathis is."

No one had ever said I could be a writer, much less just assumed it. The idea had never even crossed my mind. It wouldn't be until after college that this notion would seem like a possibility.

"I'm thirsty. You wanna go to the store and get something to drink?" I said.

"Yeah, but you didn't answer me, grasshopper. You have to promise."

"Okay, I promise."

"Thanks, bro. That wasn't so hard, now was it? And one more thing, make sure to make me good looking. You can even straighten out my chipped tooth if you want."

"You're a mess. Let's go."

"But don't change my stubby thumbs," he said, laughing. "They've done alright by me."

As I followed him to my truck, I tried to memorize the way the muscles of his back moved beneath his white undershirt, how elegantly he could stroll even when he wore shoes one size too big. His hair was short but full, and his face, even though it had been busted up in past fights, still had all the symmetry Hollywood might look for when casting for the part of the leading man in the story of your life.

KUNG FU WAS Jackie's favorite television show. He saw himself as a person of incredible knowledge whose time had come and gone. Not having a high school diploma was one of Jackie's greatest disappointments. His house was full of novels he had read and books on natural history, science, medicine, anything he could get his hands on. If he had gone to college, I think he would have become an architect or an engineer. I often wonder how different the bridges I cross and the buildings I enter would appear if his imagination had burrowed through their blueprints.

He often told me that the only chance he had to redeem his life, a life he measured as worthless, was to teach me everything he knew about people and the world so that I could protect myself and maybe realize my potential in a way that he never would.

Because Jackie was a gifted athlete in football, baseball, and track, like a handful of his other high school teammates, Jackie didn't have to try very hard in his classes. "There were some classes we didn't even have to attend," he said, as I looked in my refrigerator for some soda. I told him that some of my high school teachers who were coaches were not easy. Once, when Jackie showed up on the first day of class, he said the teacher told him to go to the gym and not return for the rest of the school year.

"What would you do in the gym, Jack?"

"The coaches would set up movies for us to watch and give us popcorn."

"Movies? Are you serious?"

"No bullshit. All day every day," he said, as he licked the paper he had rolled into a joint.

"What grade did you get in the class?"

"An A. I got an A in all of them. We all did."

"Wow. That must have been nice. I'm jealous."

"We all had a good time and got to have fun, but where did it get me? The school got touchdowns, and I became a dope head. They were using me, but I couldn't see it, Mas. I was so stupid that when they told me one month before graduation that I would have to go to summer school to get the Health credit I was short, I told them, '*Fuck that*,' and never finished."

"Wait, so you never graduated?"

"Nope. They wouldn't give me the grade, because there weren't any more touchdowns I could trade for it. I should've known better, but I was young and stupid. All us Black kids were. If I had been white, more people at that school would've given a shit about my future."

"That sucks, Jack. What a bunch of fuckers."

He took a drag and blew the smoke into the air. His eyelids heavy, he glanced at me and said, "It ain't no thing, grasshopper. I missed my chance to get out of here, but you won't. Old Jack is gonna make sure of that."

"I don't know."

"Look at me. You're a prince."

He placed his warm hand against my neck. When I raised my head and met his eyes, he said, "You're too good for this place. You have a good heart, Mas, but you let people take advantage of it. You can't let them walk all over you. Keep letting them and one day you're gonna wake up and be just like me, angry and don't give a shit about no one, not even yourself."

My face turned red. When I looked down, his hand gripped my neck and he leaned his forehead against mine and said, "You got a good spirit. One day you'll see. You're gonna learn everything I got to teach, but the last lesson will take the longest."

"What's the last lesson?" I said as I straightened up.

"Getting rid of all the people in your life who will hold you back."

"Why will that one take a long time?"

"Because some of those people will love you. And you're going to love them back. And won't want to let them go."

"Like who? Like my dad?"

"Yeah. He's one. I'm one too."

"You? Why you?"

"Because I'm no good, Mas. After I teach you everything I know, I can only hold you back. The places you're going, there's no place for an old crackhead like me."

"Then I don't want to go to those places."

"Oh, young grasshopper, only a prince would say that. It's all right, Jack's not going anywhere today."

I stared at the ground between my feet. It was brown. The yard was almost dead, and winter would be here soon.

"Don't look sad. Come on, set up the chessboard. Show me what you've learned about the knight."

"Okay."

"I'll even give you a chance and let you have the first move." He rotated the board until the white pieces were sitting in front of me.

"Alright, grasshopper, school's in session. Let's see what you have for old Jack."

WHEN I WAS in high school, I thought about changing my last name. When I was alone, I tried out what could be my new name:
Tomás Quintana

Tomás Quintana
Tomás Quintana

It didn't feel right. When I looked at it on the page, it felt like a house with the front door left open.

In the end, I figured, for better or worse, till death do us part, I was who I was. I didn't want to miss out on all the mispronunciations, either. I've heard pretty much every variation of Tomás: Toe-muss, Tuh-mahz, Toe-mosh, Too-mas. They all make me chuckle inside, except for Thomas. I let all the others fly, but that one I will correct. Unless I'm at a restaurant and I've just spelled it for the hostess who heard me say T-o-m-a-s and still wrote T-h-o-m-a-s. I give her a pass so I don't become the jerk at table 12 whose food she tells the chef to season with "something special."

My last name is even harder to pronounce. Because the *r* is between vowels, it softens and takes on the sound of a *d* so that you get something like Mo-deen—only, the *n* almost disappears. Sometimes I can barely pronounce it correctly myself.

The oddness of Morín comes from its French root that means "little Moor" or "a little moor." At some point, an ancestor who lived in France was either a small Moorish person or someone with all the wild and bristling energy of a bog. It's a toss up, because while some might laugh at the latter, there are times when I'll be so engrossed with a poem that I'll forget to comb my hair and change my clothes. During those stretches, I'm sure I've looked and smelled pretty swampy to people at the grocery store. Because Tomás means "twin," I am the Twin Swamp. To Jackie, I was mostly Mas, which means "more" in Spanish.

When I've lost my way in life and I ask Jackie for advice, in my mind his answer starts with either "Mas" or "grasshopper," a nickname he borrowed from *Kung Fu*. Sometimes our conversation lasts five minutes; other times, twenty. I close my eyes and let him speak for as long as he wants. He never stops teaching me. Even talking to him in this way, I've learned that I've always had it in me to love what isn't real.

MY FRIENDS AND I were watching *Enter the Dragon* when one of our own stumbled in. His face was bloody and broken. His lips were the size of a dish sponge. He mumbled that he had been walking home when some guys had jumped him. The walls swelled with our anger. I had only been in one fight. In sixth grade I had kicked a friend seven times who was annoying me on the playground. It barely qualified as a fight, since he hadn't hit me back. If someone had beaten up my little brother, I would have wanted to fight them. But my little brother was lost to me, like the rest of my family. I had turned my back on all of them after my grandfather had died.

Like my family, I was a walking reminder of everything good he had stood for. I didn't want to look in the mirror and remember him anymore. Whenever I did catch myself looking in the mirror for too long, it was painful. In time, I greased my hair and slicked it back, wore black on black on black, and helped my friends steal. I had become a shadow that wanted to be free from the figure of my grandfather. In my mind he loomed like granite, pink, still freckled with life. From the dirty grass, I stretched thin and away, while he cut the dazzled sky in two like he had always done.

I could feel my life begin to split. Inside, I was a busted mirror. I was no one and anyone, so much so that on that night, I became one of 8,988 minors arrested for a violent crime in Texas that year. Each of us was a piece of broken glass. In the United States, I was one of 139,120 shards. Each of us was between the ages of ten and seventeen. Each of us would answer to the charge of murder or non-negligent manslaughter or forcible rape or robbery or aggravated assault. In a few years, politicians and political scientists would call us "super-predators" and "wolf packs" and say we suffered from "moral poverty."

If a mirror broke in our house, we would have made the sign of the cross and tossed it in the trash. Over the next few weeks, before I was arrested and jailed, I wondered if I belonged in the trash too. Where I came from, no one fixed a broken mirror. And if I could be reattached to the people who loved me, would they even want me? Or would they be glad to be rid of me, since all I had been reflecting was the dark that was there and the dark that was not.

THE POLICE ARRESTED me outside a gas station. It was just one block down from the church where I had made my first communion. Across the street from the church was the bakery where my grandfather bought me the cinnamon rolls I craved. Two blocks in another direction, the tiny mom-and-pop convenience store where my grandmother and I ate snow cones, coconut for her, watermelon for me.

I could play geographic hopscotch all over Mathis and never fail to find some happy moment. Just a few years before, my eighth-grade history teacher had selected me as the All-American Boy of 1988. I thought I knew what that said about me and what I believed. And yet there I was, handcuffed in the back of a police car. In the years to come, when I became a part of the rising tide of violent crime in the United States, my history teacher would be more right in choosing me than he could have ever imagined.

I can't remember riding in the police car to the station. Even though I had driven that stretch of road to Sinton more times than I could count, the night was a blur. The seats in the cruiser were tan, and the legroom was tight in the back. The cops wore cowboy hats to let you know they were the good guys. But didn't everyone wear cowboy hats in westerns? Their shoulders were broad. They asked me questions, but I kept saying, "I plead the Fifth," because that's what people did on TV.

The first cop I had said that to put me in the back of the cruiser and said to his partner, "Do you know what that little son of a bitch just told me?"

From behind the tinted window, I saw my mom pull up and look for an officer to talk to. After she heard the charges, her face broke like a pie dropped on the ground.

When I saw her next, we were at the police station, and I had already confessed. All but one of my friends had done the same. Because I had stopped pleading the Fifth and cooperated, I was released into my mom's custody on the promise she would take me in the morning to the juvenile detention center.

I thought I had caught a break, because I didn't have to spend the night in the county lockup. But then we drove into Mathis toward my grandmother's house, and I felt like puking. Seeing my grandmother was the last thing I wanted to do, because it meant I could no longer run from what I had done or from the person I had become. When I saw her, her face said it all. She said all the things I expected her to say, the "What were you thinkings?" and the "How could you be so stupids?" I had been ready for those, but not for what she didn't say.

That night, I learned not only that love was an animal that could be kicked and punched but that it sometimes didn't heal right. For the next two years until she died, I watched her love limp around me. It would flinch when I came close. I couldn't blame her. I would've done the same if she had run me over too.

WHEN I FINISHED filling out my paperwork, the guard took me on a tour of the facility. If you ignored the fence and rolls of razor wire, the building could be mistaken from the outside for a post office or the kind of place you might buy a water softener.

Inside, the common area contained tables and chairs filled with visitors one day and teachers the next. It was the state of Texas's way of making sure we kept up with our studies. Off of this room were two doors. One led to the wing for girls; the other, for boys.

In the hallway, the steel door closed behind us, and the drowsy guard opened a plastic bag and said, "Strip."

After I placed all my clothes in the bag, he searched me to make sure I hadn't hidden any drugs or weapons in my body. When he was satisfied, I climbed into my oversize orange jumpsuit and out of the cold air.

I followed him down a narrow hallway to the showers. Each of the thick metal doors we passed had round windows that reminded me of portholes. As the guard explained the rules of the shower, the back of my neck tightened like a fist. Over my shoulder, I saw one of the round windows fill with the face of a boy about my age. His black hair was slicked back the same way I had been combing mine in the months since my grandfather had died. He smashed his nose against the glass, grinned, and then mouthed, "You. Are. Mine."

The guard said, "Do you understand?" for what felt like the hundredth time that day.

"Yes, sir."

As he walked me back up the hallway, I looked for the face in the window but only found darkness and the last of the boy's breath fading from the glass.

WHENEVER A PERSON in a movie steps into a jail cell, the camera often doesn't follow the character. Instead, on the side of freedom, the camera waits to capture the moment with as much drama as possible when the barred door shuts between the audience and the new prisoner. In order to better emphasize the barrier that now exists, the sound the door makes when it closes is amplified. Even though I had heard this clang on TV shows many times, I was not prepared. The sound I heard contained nothing of the electronic resonance you hear when a microphone filters the sound and then sends it back to you through speakers.

When the door shut behind me, it was like train cars coupling. The slam of metal on metal made a hard, low boom that vibrated the bones of my chest. A chill rushed through my body.

Later that night, I felt that chill once more after the lights went out. On my concrete bed, I was like a fish I had once caught, a wet rainbow whose guts I had scooped out with my fingers.

Alone, but not alone, in a dark room full of boys, I stared at the gray ceiling. When the sound of their breathing faded, I kept listening. Soon the hum of the building's machinery faded too. With nothing left to hear, I imagined my grandfather's thick, raspy laugh turning into a happy wheeze, a sound I hadn't heard or thought about since he died. Not ready to pray to God again, I prayed to my grandfather instead. Having confessed everything I had done and begged forgiveness, I drifted off and slept better than I had in months.

THE NEXT MORNING as we lined up for the head count before breakfast, I met the face in the window. Leaning over my shoulder, he whispered in my ear that he was going to fuck me up. When I ignored him, he asked where I was from. When he heard Mathis, he said, "Were you in that crew pinched yesterday?"

"What about it?" I reluctantly nodded.

He sized me up, tried to determine how much of my attitude was true toughness and how much was bullshit.

"What's your name?"

"Tomás Morín."

When he heard Morín, his eyes sparkled.

"Is your father Joe Morín, El Indio?"

"Yeah, do you know him?"

"Shit, everybody knows Indio." With that, his scowl vanished, and a genuine, warm smile crawled across his face like a spider.

"If anyone wants to mess with you, they're going to have to go through me first."

As I thanked my new friend, I realized that for the first time in sixteen years, I had traded on my father's name for the respect and admiration of a stranger. It would also be the last time.

I TOLD MY mom on the phone not to visit me in jail, that I didn't want her to see me like that, to get the image of me behind bars stuck in her head. But that was a lie.

I was a coward.

The real reason was because I couldn't see her heart break anymore than it already had. If I did, I would've lost it. I was afraid my cellmates would think I was weak if they saw me crying. Instead, I asked her to tell my father I wanted to see him, a man she hadn't spoken to in six years.

As I watched the guards process my father, I scanned his face for a sign of what he might be thinking. He seemed larger than what I remembered. His chest was wide and thick, and the guards looked weak next to him. For a second, I imagined him breaking me out and driving us off into a new life where it would just be the two of us. We would change our names, and he would finally teach me how to be a bricklayer so we could build houses together.

When we hugged, he held me the way you hold the bag after you've cleaned up what your dog left on the sidewalk.

"Do you want to sit down?" He stared at me and then followed as I led us to a table. The other kids pretended to play checkers or talk in the corner. A visit from one of our parents was what we all said we wanted.

"Your momma said you wanted to see me."

"I told her to ask you. Thanks for coming."

"How are you, mijo?"

"Okay, I guess."

"Boy, how stupid could you be? What's wrong with you?"

"I don't know."

"You and your friends could've killed somebody. Your momma is worried sick about you."

I stared at the table between us and wondered how many minutes of our visit had gone by and how many were left before he would be asked to leave and I could go back to my cell.

The fantasy that he would rescue me was gone. There would be no changing our identities. He wouldn't shave his mustache and hide me in Colorado or Wyoming or anywhere the fishing was good. I now knew that come what may, he would always be himself and I would always be me.

"You have it nice in here, boy. This is like a playpen. You don't want to be in prison like me. You better straighten your life out before you end up somewhere worse than this."

"I know. I'm going to try."

In the six years since my mom had kicked him out, he had settled back in across town with the wife and kids he had left for my mom. I wondered what my half brothers and half sisters thought of me, the son of the "other woman."

He was right that I was a moron. Not just for everything I had done, but also for asking to see him in the first place, because the person I had really wanted to see was Jackie, the man who had been not just the father I needed but the father I had always wanted.

I can't remember every word Jackie said to me when he visited a few days later. He probably talked about how my mom and little brother were doing. I'm sure I asked him what people were saying about me around town. He probably asked me if anyone was giving me any trouble and if I was staying on top of my homework.

Even though none of those memories stuck, what I do remember is his smile and how warm his hand felt when he gripped my shoulder and said, "I believe in you, Mas. You're gonna be alright. Look at me. I know you, and this isn't you. Not inside where it counts. We're gonna get through this, alright?"

I never forgot those words or that hand and smile. They made me cry that day. I cried while he was talking with me, and I didn't care who might be watching or what it might mean for later.

I wish I could remember what I said when someone asked me who that man was. Did I say he was my dad or my friend? Whatever came out of my mouth, I'm sure the right answer was written all over my face.

Throughout the next couple of weeks of my detention, my short trial, and the year of probation that followed, that moment stayed with me. For many years, I believed he was teaching me about loyalty on that day. I couldn't have been more wrong. The lesson was about forgiveness, the true kind, the Jesus-type kind some people don't think exists anymore. That and how I still didn't know the first thing about it.

THE DAY I RETURN to school, I feel like everyone can see the ankle monitoring bracelet I've hidden under my jeans. I don't really belong to myself anymore. I can only go from home to school. I belong to my probation officer, which means for the next year San Patricio County, and thus the state of Texas and all its police officers, owns me.

I've been in the county juvenile detention center for two weeks. Whom do people see when I walk down the hall? Am I dark and mysterious like my father? Or am I a cartoon villain, a shadow with ridiculous feet and cherry tomatoes for eyes?

IN ART CLASS, I knew I could escape from my life for at least an hour, because drawing had helped me forget I was in juvie. When my teacher called me Jailbird, the paper in front of me began to close like a door. I knew then that no matter what I had drawn or what my teacher had said, that paper would have always been a door because I had made it. I had built it out of anger. It was heavy and had no handle. There was no place to slide in a key either. It could only open if someone pushed it from the other side.

My classmates were quiet. When I looked at my teacher, he chuckled. His face was an overripe strawberry. After class a girl I liked held my hand and whispered, "Bad boy." Her soft face blushed. I didn't know life could be like that.

WHEN MY GEOMETRY teacher said, "Welcome back. Did you get the homework I sent you?" I was not prepared for the uneasy warmth in the way he said the word "welcome." Maybe he hoped the kid returning to his class was the same as the one who had been there just two weeks prior. I didn't want to be the person I was two weeks ago. I wanted to push further back to a year, before my grandfather had died, when I still hadn't replaced my friends with new ones who liked trouble, before I started wearing trench coats and black clothes, before I started combing my hair back until it looked like a wet scab.

"Yes, sir, I did."

"We'll get you caught up as soon as we can."

I drew an equilateral triangle. I measured and remeasured every side. The day felt tied to its symmetry.

There was no room for mistakes anymore. Outside our classroom, the line of trouble waiting for me was infinite. I stared at the graph paper until my classmates, the room, even my desk blurred green and white and became a sheet of flypaper I could land on and prove I was still worthy of a life.

SOME DAYS, I feel my father wake inside me. A car is left unlocked. A woman walks by with her purse open. As far as I know, my father never stole anything. Jackie was the one who stole when he felt he was justified. Someone once owed him money, so he took a box of tools from their garage as payment.

It's the weakness of others that makes my father waken inside of me and lift his head. He sees their weakness and how it leaves them vulnerable. He sees all the angles, the ways in which he can get ahead. He whispers all of this to me. I've asked him to stop, but he ignores me.

"Life is a country of pain, and I know how to read the map," he says.

He wants to lead me through the mountains, down a pass to a place beside a lake where no one lives. We can fish and swim there. The others who are like him are waiting at every turn, will hurt me if they have a chance, and will take what I have and make it their own.

"Why do you keep showing me all of this?" I ask him.

Like a good guide, he keeps his eyes ahead, watching for danger. He doesn't look back, because he knows I can only follow since his legs are my legs.

Jackie could see the pain of the world too. He knew its trails. Together we walk toward it and smile. He points out the dangerous people in the trees, calls them monkeys, and teaches me to laugh at them. "Always watch them," he says. I try to never let those people out of my sight. "They smile in your face, but behind your back they want to take your place," he says.

Some days, my father and Jackie are the same man. I listen to the music of their voices, and I can't tell them apart. They both sound as hollow as a coffin, their throats lined in satin.

I haven't heard Jackie's voice in months. I miss the way his grin breaks across my mind. I want him to tell me something about my life, to tell me I'm doing okay. He never told me when I would stop needing to hear that.

He taught me how to be one of the broken people that my father taught me to move around. How lucky is the son who can say each of his fathers showed him how to do what they knew best?

I guess Jackie's lesson was that not all men will break my heart and sell the pieces. And even when they do, as he would years down the road, it could be gentle and loving. I'm still trying to figure out how that works.

A '66 MUSTANG was the first car Jackie and I ever worked on. A hunter-green coupe, it didn't have a speck of rust on the chrome bumpers, badges, or trim. While the exterior was a conversation starter, what was under the hood, and behind the shiny panels, needed mending, since most of the parts had been set in place on the factory floor a decade before I was born.

I can't remember how we found the Mustang Graveyard in Kingsville. On the lot there was a mechanic shop the size of a barn, with spare parts hung on every wall. Outside, row after row of old Mustangs waited under the Texas sun for someone to pull their parts and give them a new life.

As we walked, we called out the year and model of each car: fastback, coupe, convertible, vinyl top. Hubcaps, side vents, gas caps, they all gave clues about the birthday and design of each car. We poked our heads inside one car and saw the two-tone pony interior with its scene of two herds of horses running and stomping toward one another.

Back home, with all the parts we needed to rebuild my front end, under the shade of a mesquite tree, we began. After the tire was off, we took stock of the upper and lower control arms, tie rods, the rusty springs taut with tension, and the bushings, all of which, when replaced, would keep my car not just from creaking and groaning but also from drifting side to side whenever I drove across the slightest rise or hit a hole in the road.

For this job, we needed two jacks and a lot of luck. No professional mechanic will do front-end work without a spring compressor, because the risk is too high that something will go wrong. Not having one, we used one jack to lift the car and another to compress the spring. While it was compressed, we ran a couple of chains through the spring and secured them with padlocks so that when we lowered the jack that had compressed the spring, the chains would keep it from expanding back out.

"Alright, Mas, go hide while I lower the jack."

"Sure thing, Jack."

"No, farther. Get behind the car. I once heard a dude tried this and the chain popped."

"Fuck."

"The spring hit him in the chest and killed him just like that."

We both agreed that the fatal mistake of the guy in the story who died was choosing to stand in front of the spring, so Jackie crawled on his stomach until he was within arm's reach of the jack handle.

The jack hissed as it lowered. No spring flew out from under the fender of my car like a missile. We angled the spring and worked it out from the car. It vibrated in our hands like a living thing. We placed it behind a shed where we thought it would be safe to explode if the chains broke. After we had replaced all the parts on the right side of the front end, it was time to reinsert the spring. It was my job to raise the jack under the control arm so that while the spring was compressed, Jackie could release the padlock and slip the chains out. My hands dripped with sweat, and my body shivered from fear, as Jackie kneeled in front of the spring and set it back in place. One mistake on my part and Jackie could die.

Once the spring was reinstalled, we laughed. The left side of the front end should have been smooth sailing, but it wasn't. The other spring had a hairline crack. It was small, but Jackie said if the spring failed while I was driving, I could wreck my car or worse. While it only took us a couple of days to find a replacement spring, the problem we couldn't solve was what to do with the faulty spring once it was compressed and padlocked with nowhere to go. In the end, we placed it behind the shed. We stared at the spring for a few long seconds as the chains vibrated with its energy.

Over twenty years have passed, and I still think about that spring, wondering if anyone with better sense than us found it and used a spring compressor to release it safely or if it just exploded one day and tore a hole through the shed wall or just flew into the meadow of the empty lot next door. Or maybe it's still there, its chains rusty, worn from holding back what was meant to be free.

IN 1995 WHEN I drove Jackie to Austin to reconnect with his family, he was happier than at almost any other time I had seen him. What I didn't know was that I would soon lose the last of my fathers. One year later, he finally succeeded at kicking me out of his life and avoiding his greatest fear, that I would ruin my life by associating with him, with a man who couldn't control the needs of his body.

His plan was so simple, so Jackie.

While he was visiting me at my college apartment one summer, he took my then girlfriend's car without permission during the night. When I woke up the next morning and found him gone, I saw that the space next to my car was empty. His bet was that when I phoned her at her conference in the Midwest and told her what had happened, she would want me to file a police report. Even though her car would be found a day later by the Austin Police Department in front of the house of Jackie's sister, he knew what would happen next—my girlfriend would ask me to choose between him and her.

I can't recall if she did ask me to do just that. What I do remember is feeling like I needed to make amends or I would lose her. He gambled that I would see his sacrifice and do the right thing and let him go.

When he died in November 2013, shortly before Thanksgiving, we hadn't seen or spoken to one another in seventeen years.

JACKIE WAS TALLER than me. That's what I remember. The old Polaroid in my hand says differently. After twenty years, the mind can trick you. In the picture, we are in someone's driveway, part dirt, part concrete. A flatbed work truck is in the background. It could be a small tow truck at first glance, because it has a boom winch to pull up a car like many of the hook-and-chain-type tow trucks popular in the eighties. There are no slings or mats for the wheels of a car to rest against, so I don't know exactly what I'm looking at.

One of Jackie's many odd jobs was to transport and block mobile homes for a local company. He would often drive the toter, the giant of the tow trucks. Toters resemble the semis that pull trailers all over the country. The man who owned that company also owned a mechanic shop where Jackie moonlighted. The dark-green coveralls Jackie is wearing might mean we are at this mechanic shop.

My Ford Ranger is parked behind the tow truck with the winch. Someone had parked their car close behind my truck. I think they knew my truck, knew they wouldn't be blocking me in, because wherever Jackie was, so was I.

Jackie and I are in the same pose. We stand side by side, pointing at the camera with our right index fingers. The graduation ring I'm wearing means it's 1994, my senior year of high school. We only have a couple of years left before we never see or speak to each other again.

"When someone wants to take your picture, you point at them like this to let them know you're a bad mamma jamma. When you point at them, they *know*, and you *know* that they know. That's how you do it, grasshopper," he said, just before the shutter shut its mouth.

THE CASE BROUGHT by the world was as follows:

Name: Jackie Eugene Powell. The first name derives from John, the English version of Yochanan, which means "God's grace" in Hebrew. His middle name in Greek means "well born." Some sources argue Powell is a form of Paul, which means "small."

Alias: Rabbit. Most from Mathis assumed that this name came from his constant search for dope or for his jitteriness when he was high. His cousin said the name was born when Jackie wore a pair of underwear on his head like a crown while he had sex with a woman faster than anyone in the room had ever seen.

Charges: The court of the world brought the following against Jackie.

possession of crack
absent father
shoplifting
resentful son
lust
possession of cocaine
speeding
failure to pay taxes
gluttony
driving under the
    influence
jaywalking
idolatry
failure to pay child
    support
envy

distant husband
aggravated assault
pride
entering a store with
    no shoes
lying
grand theft auto
sloth
forgery
possession of marijuana
fraud
greed
public intoxication
plagiarism
insurance fraud
anger

Verdict: Guilty.
Sentence: Hunger. Sorrow. Ridicule. Loneliness. Cancer. A
potter's field in Manor, Texas, where he found his green crown
and went into the world that would not have him as its Rabbit
king.

LONG AFTER MY mom had kicked my father out, I saw Jackie
steal food from the grocery store. Sometimes he stole so he could
trade the food for drugs; other times, he stole to eat, because he
was hungry. Since his house didn't have electricity, there was
no refrigerator to keep anything cold. Most of the time, he ate
peanut butter or bummed meals off friends.

Whether he stole for drugs or hunger, he said he never felt
bad about stealing from the grocery store.

"What do you mean they have it coming, Jack?"

"I've told the manager before that they should donate all that food they throw in the trash. There's lots of hungry people who need it. But they don't listen. All they want to do is protect the owners. And do you think the owners give a fuck, with all their millions of dollars a year they make?"

"You told them that? When?"

"Lots of times, but they didn't listen. So I just take what I want, because it's probably going to end up in the trash anyway, so why not pick it up early?"

"What if they catch you? They could send you to jail."

"They're not gonna stop me. And if they do call the police and send me to jail, then I'll get three hot meals a day for a couple of weeks. Either way, I get to eat. That's called checkmate, grasshopper."

I couldn't help but smile and laugh when his eyes glimmered like that. For a brief second, they would brighten just like a light bulb flickers and glows before it pops and burns out.

"This one time, I walked straight back to the store's meat section and put the biggest T-bone down the front of my shorts. As I was walking out the front, the manager kept saying, 'Sir. Sir . . . Please stop, sir.' I just kept walking. You should've seen his face. While I was cooking the steak over the fire at home, one of the cops walked into the yard and said, 'What are you doing?' I told him I was about to have dinner and asked if he wanted to join me. He just laughed and told me to stay out of H-E-B from now on."

Jackie wore the clothes and shoes other people didn't want. He found food where and when he could. Even his books were borrowed. I didn't know anyone who got so much use out of everything they owned. Nothing seemed wasted, except his life.

WE WORE OUT Santana's greatest hits, the album with the dove on the cover that makes people mad because the solos are cut out of some of the songs. *Chill Out* by John Lee Hooker too. On "Hear My Train a Comin'," Jimi Hendrix sings,

> Waitin' for that train
> Take me home
> From this lonesome place . . .

IN THE WINTER, after nightfall, when I looked out my window across the street, the fire Jackie would build in his backyard was like the distant light of a train moving through the dark that I longed to catch.

In the summer, he kept the fires going to heat the large tractor disc he had welded to a stand. Once he had the Coors Light he had mixed with a little oil bubbling, he would slip some tripas he had peppered and salted into the disc. It was like a giant wok. There was even enough room to lay corn tortillas along the side above the oil so that when the tripas were brown and crispy, we could fork them into a hot tortilla and feast on tripe tacos.

At home I studied a book on chess openings, on how to properly finish an opponent when you only had a queen and a rook or a bishop or a knight. Or two pawns. The variations were infinite, but the end was the same, if you were patient and made the right moves. It would take me seven years before I would beat Jackie in chess for the first time.

We played chess and basketball day after day. Even now, I can see him studying the board, his eyes locked on all the possibilities I can't see, while his hand, index finger extended, moves like a conductor's over the board the way it did when he had made up his mind about what piece to move.

If we were in the middle game, he would set his piece down, dramatically pull his hand away and look at me with mischief in his eyes, shimmy his head a little, and say, "Think on that, grasshopper, while I go take a leak."

While he disappeared into the tall weeds at the edge of his yard, I would stare at the board, flustered. Sometimes, while he was rolling a cigarette or turning up the radio in my truck, I would go to his side to try and see through his eyes, but it didn't work, because I could never see what he had in store for me.

At first, we played on a card table he would set under a tree. Eventually, he found us an aluminum table that sat on a black pole from which four aluminum stools jutted out. Even though he had spray-painted a chessboard on the table—half the squares were blue and the other half were the dull silver of the table—we rarely ever used it, because it was too hard to keep clean and the color had faded anyway.

Until I had enough money to buy us a new set, we used one he had that was missing a white pawn. Because we would eventually lose whatever we had used in place of the pawn in the last game (a nickel, a cigarette filter, a die), we would have to find something new.

The thin aluminum stools of our table were low to the ground and narrow like the ones in the visitor's center of the county jail. Once, during my first summer break from college, my mom and I went to visit Jackie in the county jail. The room was a large half circle with the visitors on one side and the inmates on the other.

While I waited for Jackie to be brought out, I heard a guard on the other side call out, "Joe Morín!" I froze for a moment, unsure of what was happening. Then my mind twitched. How could they have gotten confused? Why would they bring my father to see me? What was he doing there to begin with? Then I remembered I hadn't written my father's name on the inmate-request log. There was no way they could know that Joe Morín was my father. When I looked around, I saw her, my father's wife. How many times had my brother and I called her a witch when we were kids? How many times had we unfairly blamed her for my father dividing his attention between their children and us?

I waved at my father when he came out to see his wife.

As I watched my father through the plastic that separated them, I noticed that his facial expression was no different than what I remembered. He was completely calm in spite of the fact he was in jail. If he had asked me to get him a beer from the kitchen, even though he hadn't lived with us for years, the memory stored in my muscles of that simple, meaningful request likely would've made me start to rise from my seat. If only he had said that, then I would've gotten to see him smile and laugh at the joke. But he didn't. His usual who-are-we-burying-today face was on tight.

Then the guard called out, "Jackie Powell!"

I knew my father didn't like him. He had said as much when he heard rumors that Jackie and I had been seen together a lot after my mom kicked my father out of the house.

When Jackie came to another window to speak to me, he was all smiles and acted like he was ready to play a leisurely game of chess. I can't recall why he was in jail. This could very well be one of the times when he stole something and let himself get caught because, as he always pointed out, at least in jail he'd get fed and have somewhere cool to sleep.

When he sat down, I joked about how the white uniform looked good on him. We talked about how my father was there, and just before the usual awkwardness we felt when my father or Jackie's sons were around, the guard yelled, "Powell, the judge wants to see you."

He perked up and said, "Don't leave yet, Mas. I might be getting out!"

"I know, Jack. My mom went to talk to the judge about getting you released on your own recognizance."

"For real?"

"Yup. I'll meet you outside."

As I watched him walk away, I turned and saw that the chair across from my father was empty now. I reluctantly walked over to his stall. His face was like an empty swimming pool in fall.

"Hey, Dad. How's it going?"

"It's okay, mijo. What are you doing here? I thought you were at school."

"I am. But I'm home for the summer break."

"It's good to see you, boy. Are you getting good grades?"

I told him I was on the honor roll and had made a lot of new friends. I told him that college was nothing like high school, that it was better. He was happy to hear I had at last found somewhere I fit in. When he asked if I thought about trying out for the cross-country team, I told him that between studying and working, I didn't have the time or energy. He nodded.

I didn't know what else to say. While he stared at me, the inmates and their families in all the stalls around us chatted easily. Their voices were laced with hope. I could see a warmth in his eyes that I hadn't noticed when I had first sat down. Was he happy to see me in spite of the fact I had come to the county jail to visit Jackie? Or was this how he showed his pride at the news that I was thriving in college? I didn't want to ask him any of the questions I heard from the other stalls: *How is the food? Do you have enough to read? Is there any good news from your lawyer? Is anyone messing with you? Are you sleeping okay?*

I didn't want to ask those questions because I knew that whatever answers he gave, those answers wouldn't matter. He had been in jail before and probably would be again. He would get out when it was time, and that was that. We had never been good at small talk, and we weren't about to start now.

"Well, I gotta go. Mom and Juan are waiting for me."

"Okay. Take care of yourself. I love you, mijo."

"I love you too."

It was hard to see my father in jail. He looked like a dog chained to a tree after only ever having run through fields. He had sat at the window of the world's car for so long as it sped along, oblivious to the other passengers, the air crashing against his teeth and filling his gums and ears up until it looked like he might catch enough wind to take flight.

Outside, we met Jackie. When he hugged my mom to thank her for arranging his release, she gripped her purse and yelled, "Help me! Thief!"

"Bert, cut it out! You're gonna get me thrown back in there," he said, as we all laughed.

As I drove us home, no one said much. The world was right again and, for once, fair. I didn't know what came next, but I was sure the future was filled with many more days like this, moments when we would forget about what we couldn't change in our lives. As ranches and cows stretched out ahead of us outside of town, I pushed the gas pedal and made my Mustang hug the curves. On the downhills, we dove and rose, until we lost our breath and didn't care if we ever found it again.

On Names Again

I love thee freely, as men strive for right;
I love thee purely, as they turn from praise.

blasphemy (sixth century): He who wants to grapple with the demon of blasphemy in any other way is like a man trying to hold lightning in his hands. For how will you catch, or contend and grapple with one who bursts into the heart suddenly like the wind, utters words quicker than a flash, and immediately vanishes? He who despises this foe is delivered from its torture. But he who contrives some other way to wage war with it will end by submitting to it. He who wishes to conquer the spirits with words is like one trying to lock up the winds.
   —*The Ladder of Divine Ascent* by St. John Climacus,
      translated by Archimandrite Lazarus Moore

scrupulosity (1471): The scrupulous are to act against their scruples, and plant their feet firmly in resisting them. We cannot set scruples to rest better than by despising them. They are like a pack of dogs who bark and snap at passers-by; the best way to deal with them is to ignore them and treat them with contempt.

— *Tractatus de remediis contra pusillanimitatem scrupulositatem* by Jean Charlier de Gerson

scrupolisity (1477): A scruple is a state of indecision and fear arising from improbable conjectures. Scrupolisity is equivalent to pusillanimity. The five causes are: a weak constitution, mental illness, the devil, excess in ascetical practices, association with scrupulous persons.

— *Summa Theologica Moralis* by St. Antoninus

melancholy (1621): Pacify them for one, they are instantly troubled with some other fear; always afraid of something which they foolishly imagine or conceive to themselves, which never peradventure was, never can be, never likely will be; . . . which so much, so continually tortures and crucifies their souls, like a barking dog that always bawls, but seldom bites, this fear ever molesteth, and so long as melancholy lasteth, cannot be avoided.

— *The Anatomy of Melancholy* by Robert Burton

scruples (1660): A Scruple is a great Trouble of Mind proceeding from a little Motive, and a great Indisposition, by which the Conscience, though sufficiently determined by proper Arguments, dares not proceed to Action,—or if it do, it cannot rest. Scruple is a little stone in the foot; if you set it upon the ground, it hurts you; if you hold it up, you cannot go forward; it is a trouble where the trouble is over, a doubt when doubts are resolved.

— *The Whole Works of the Right Rev. Jeremy Taylor* by Jeremy Taylor

melancholy (1755): 1) A disease, supposed to proceed from a redundance of black bile; but it is better known to arise from too heavy and too viscid blood: its cure is in evacuation, nervous medicines, and powerful stimuli. 2) A kind of madness, in which the mind is always fixed on one object. 3) A gloomy, pensive, discontented temper.

—*A Dictionary of the English Language* by Samuel Johnson

reasoning monomania (1838): Patients, affected with this variety of insanity, have in truth, a partial delirium. They perform acts, and hold odd, strange and absurd conversations, which they regard as such, and for which they censure themselves. The signs of reasoning monomania, consist in the change and perversion of the habits, disposition and affections.

—*Mental Madness: A Treatise on Insanity* by E. Esquirol, translated by E. K. Hunt

melancholy (1845): They are commonly exceeding fearful, causelessly or beyond what there is cause for: every thing which they hear or see is ready to increase their fears, especially if fear was the first cause, as ordinarily it is. Their thoughts are most upon themselves, like the millstones that grind on themselves, when they have no grist: so one thought begets another.

—*The Practical Works of Richard Baxter* by Richard Baxter

evil thoughts (1848): The form of tribulation under discussion is agonisingly painful and moreover dialectically complicated to the point of madness; it is, if one could imagine it thus in order to define it theologically: an educational torture which, if nothing else, is calculated to extinguish all self-will. [T]o try to forget and to avoid them, does not help; for that is exactly what he does and it only brings dread nearer. In his impatience it will seem as though not even children torturing a butterfly could inflict such pain.

—*The Journals of Soren Kierkegaard* by Soren Kierkegaard, translated by Alexander Dru

Zwangsvorstellungen (1867): To the degree that a [compulsive thought] imposes itself ever more strongly and frequently, it enforces its influence upon the will, a matter that even in healthy individuals essentially constricts the action of free choice, but in illness must turn the patient into a pure automaton.

—*Contributions to the Recognition and Correct Forensic Assessment of Diseased Mental States, for Physicians, Judges, and Defender* by Dr. Richard von Krafft-Ebing

Grubelnsucht (1868): A ruminatory or questioning illness (from the Old German, Grubelen, racking one's brains).

—*Über einen wenig bekannten psychopathischen Zustand* by Dr. Wilhelm Griesinger

folie impulsive (1870): The loss of reason does not for us imply a disturbance of intelligence, what is more the individual can reason in a perfectly fine manner, without the least enjoyment of his reasoning; it is especially the facts of this nature which characterize impulsive madness.

—*Des Impulsions dans la Folie et de la Folie Impulsive* by Dr. Henri Dagonet

folie du doute/délire du toucher (1875): The phrase doubting mania (with touching mania) speaks of my clear desire to name this condition according to salient clinical features; namely, a mental questioning prompted by doubt and by fear of contact with certain external objects.

Doubt begins the morbid drama. Long afterward, eccentricities about *touching* bring the drama to a close. In giving a name to the illness, *doubt* and *touching* should be juxtaposed. This would probably be the only way of lastingly fixing one's attention on these two fundamental peculiarities of the neurosis in question.

—*La Folie du Doute avec Délire de Toucher* by Dr. Henri Le Grand du Saulle, translated by Michael H. Stone

Zwangsvorstellungen (1877): Obsessive ideas which, in the presence of intact intelligence and with no disorder of the emotional life or affect, intrude into the foreground of consciousness against the will of the concerned individual; they do not allow themselves to be banished, and they obstruct and divert the normal course of ideas. The patient sees them as abnormal and alien as he contemplates them with his healthy consciousness.

—"Über Zwangsvorstellungen" in *Berliner Klinische Wochenschrift* by Dr. Karl Westphal

imperative ideas (1894): With regard to the symptoms, they assume different forms. With some, the torment is that certain ideas or words arise with painful frequency and vividness. The thoughts which dominate the mind with morbid persistency are generally of an unusual and unwelcome character. . . . Then there are persons who invariably touch some object in passing it. . . . Then we have arithmomania, or the morbid desire to count without rhyme or reason. . . . What strikes one forcibly in regard to most, if not all, imperative ideas is that between them and ordinary ideas the difference is one of degree, and that it is a most difficult thing to determine when the boundary line has been passed.

—"Imperative Ideas" in *Brain* by Dr. Daniel Tuke

obsessions and compulsions (1903): Obsessives tend not to worry about things outside their control but rather about things within their (imagined) control. . . . These actions are generally bad, the opposite of what the patient wishes to do. Thus obsessions and compulsions often involve the thought or action that is most objectionable to the patient and causes him the most horror. . . . [Some] demonstrate a need for precision or perfection in perceptions and actions. They include manias of order and symmetry. Arithmetic manias arise because numbers are seen as precise.

Symbolism plays a large role in the malady and the mania of symbolism is also related to the need for precision, to express with sharpness feelings and ideas about which the patient is uncertain. The mania of slowness arises from the fear that an action done quickly won't be done precisely, and the mania of repetition arises from the feeling of discontent with the way an action was previously performed; as does the mania of going back (checking).

—"Obsessions and Psychasthenia: A Synopsis" of *Obsessions and Psychasthenia* by Dr. Pierre Janet, translated by Roger K. Pitman

compulsion neurosis (1912): The essence of the compulsion neurosis may be expressed in the following simple formula: Obsessions are always transformed *reproaches* returning from the repression which always refer to a pleasurably accomplished sexual action of childhood. The reason for the unassailableness of the obsession or its derivative is due only to its connection with the repressed memory of early childhood, for as soon as we succeed in making it conscious, for which the psycho-therapeutic methods already seem quite sufficient, the compulsion, too, becomes detached.

—*Selected Papers on Hysteria and Other Psychoneuroses* by Dr. Sigmund Freud, translated by A. A. Brill

obsessive compulsive reaction, 40.4 (1952): In this reaction the anxiety is associated with the persistence of unwanted ideas and of repetitive impulses to perform acts which may be considered morbid by the patient. The patient himself may regard his ideas and behavior as unreasonable, but nevertheless is compelled to carry out his rituals. The diagnosis will specify the symptomatic expression of such reactions, as touching, counting, ceremonials, hand-washing, or recurring thoughts (accompanied often by a compulsion to repetitive action). This category includes many cases formerly classified as "psychasthenia."

—*Diagnostic and Statistical Manual of Mental Disorders I*

obsessive compulsive neurosis, 300.3 (1968): This disorder is characterized by the persistent intrusion of unwanted thoughts, urges, or actions that the patient is unable to stop. The thoughts may consist of single words or ideas, ruminations, or trains of thought often perceived by the patient as nonsensical. The actions vary from simple movements to complex rituals such as repeated handwashing. Anxiety and distress are often present either if the patient is prevented from completing his compulsive ritual or if he is concerned about being unable to control it himself.

—*Diagnostic and Statistical Manual of Mental Disorders II*

obsessive compulsive disorder (or Obsessive Compulsive Neurosis), 300.30 (1980): The essential features are recurrent obsessions or compulsions. *Obsessions* are recurrent, persistent ideas, thoughts, images, or impulses that are ego-dystonic, that is, they are not experienced as voluntarily produced, but rather as thoughts that invade consciousness and are experienced as senseless or repugnant. Attempts are made to ignore or suppress them. *Compulsions* are repetitive and seemingly purposeful behaviors that are performed according to certain rules or in a stereotyped fashion. The behavior is not an end in itself, but is designed to produce or to prevent some future event or situation. However, the activity is not connected in a realistic way with what it is designed to produce or prevent, or may be clearly excessive. The act is performed with a sense of subjective compulsion coupled with a desire to resist the compulsion (at least initially). The individual generally recognizes the senselessness of the behavior (this may not be true for young children) and does not derive pleasure from carrying out the activity, although it provides a release of tension.

The most common obsessions are repetitive thoughts of violence (e.g., killing one's child), contamination (e.g., becoming infected by shaking hands), and doubt (e.g., repeatedly wondering whether one has performed some action, such as having hurt someone in a traffic accident). The most common compulsions involve hand-washing, counting, checking, and touching.

When the individual attempts to resist a compulsion, there is a sense of mounting tension that can be immediately relieved by yielding to the compulsion. In the course of the illness, after repeated failure at resisting the compulsions, the individual may give in to them and no longer experience a desire to resist them.

—*Diagnostic and Statistical Manual of Mental Disorders III*

obsessive compulsive disorder, 300.3 (2000): The essential features of Obsessive-Compulsive Disorder are recurrent obsessions or compulsions (Criterion A) that are severe enough to be time consuming (i.e., they take more than 1 hour a day) or cause marked distress or significant impairment (Criterion C). At some point during the course of the disorder, the person has recognized that the obsessions or compulsions are excessive or unreasonable (Criterion B). If another Axis I disorder is present, the content of the obsessions or compulsions is not restricted to it (Criterion D). The disturbance is not due to the direct physiological effects of a substance (e.g., a drug of abuse, a medication) or a general medical condition (Criterion E).

Obsessions are persistent ideas, thoughts, impulses, or images that are experienced as intrusive and inappropriate and that cause marked anxiety or distress. The intrusive and inappropriate quality of the obsessions has been referred to as "ego-dystonic." This refers to the individual's sense that the content of the obsession is alien, not within his or her own control, and not the kind of thought that he or she would expect to have. However, the individual is able to recognize that the obsessions are the product of his or her own mind and are not imposed from without (as in thought insertion).

The most common obsessions are repeated thoughts about contamination (e.g., becoming contaminated by shaking hands), repeated doubts (e.g., wondering whether one has performed some act such as having hurt someone in a traffic accident or having left a door unlocked), a need to have things in a particular order (e.g., intense distress when objects are disordered or asymmetrical), aggressive or horrific impulses (e.g., to hurt one's child or to shout an obscenity in church), and sexual imagery (e.g., a recurrent pornographic image). The thoughts, impulses, or images are not simply excessive worries about real-life problems (e.g., concerns about current ongoing difficulties in life, such as financial, work, or school problems) and are unlikely to be related to a real-life problem.

The individual with obsessions usually attempts to ignore or suppress such thoughts or impulses or to neutralize them with some other thought or action (i.e., a compulsion). For example, an individual plagued by doubts about having turned off the stove attempts to neutralize them by repeatedly checking to ensure that it is off.

Compulsions are repetitive behaviors (e.g., hand washing, ordering, checking) or mental acts (e.g., praying, counting, repeating words silently) the goal of which is to prevent or reduce anxiety or distress, not to provide pleasure or gratification. In most cases, the person feels driven to perform the compulsion to reduce the distress that accompanies an obsession or to prevent some dreaded event or situation. For example, individuals with obsessions about being contaminated may reduce their mental distress by washing their hands until their skin is raw; individuals distressed by obsessions about having left a door unlocked may be driven to check the lock every few minutes; individuals distressed by unwanted blasphemous thoughts may find relief in counting to 10 backward and forward 100 times for each thought. In some cases individuals perform rigid or stereotyped acts according to idiosyncratically elaborated rules without being able to indicate why they are doing them. By definition, compulsions are either clearly excessive or are not connected in a realistic way with what they are designed to neutralize or prevent. The most common compulsions involve washing and cleaning, counting, checking, requesting or demanding assurances, repeating actions, and ordering.

—*Diagnostic and Statistical Manual of Mental Disorders IV—TR*

obsessive-compulsive disorder, F42 (2013): Obsessive-compulsive and related disorders include obsessive-compulsive disorder (OCD), body dysmorphic disorder, hoarding disorder, trichotillomania (hair pulling disorder), excoriation (skin-picking) disorder, substance/medication-induced obsessive-compulsive and related disorder, obsessive-compulsive and related disorder due to another medical condition, and other specified obsessive-compulsive and related disorder and unspecified obsessive-compulsive and related disorder (e.g., body-focused repetitive behavior disorder, obsessional jealousy).

OCD is characterized by the presence of obsessions and/or compulsions. *Obsessions* are recurrent and persistent thoughts, urges, or images that are experienced as intrusive and unwanted, whereas *compulsions* are repetitive behaviors or mental acts that an individual feels driven to perform in response to an obsession or according to rules that must be applied rigidly. Some other obsessive-compulsive and related disorders are also characterized by preoccupations and by repetitive behaviors or mental acts in response to the preoccupations. Other obsessive-compulsive and related disorders are characterized primarily by recurrent body-focused repetitive behaviors (e.g., hair pulling, skin picking) and repeated attempts to decrease or stop the behaviors.

—*Diagnostic and Statistical Manual of Mental Disorders V*

Freud, like Kraepelin before him, called this entity Zwangsneu-rose; by way of different translations, Zwang became "obsession" in London and "compulsion" in New York. Subsequent authors, apparently unaware of this fact and eager to ascertain what is meant by "obsessive" and what by "compulsive," settled for the unhappy designation "obsessive-compulsive."

—*American Handbook of Psychiatry*, edited by Sandor Rado

How Do I Love Thee?

I love thee with the breath,
Smiles, tears, of all my life; and, if God choose,
I shall but love thee better after death.

It was the late nineties. At a small kitchen table in Baltimore, the minutes passed. Ten. Twenty. My friends talked about our classmates in our PhD program, the crime that was getting worse, Spain, books, and dinners. I listened happily and took everything in, dreading the question I knew would come before long, "Why aren't you saying anything?"

My friend Eva's question wasn't that blunt, but my answer was. When I said, "I prefer to only speak when I feel I have something to say," Eva and Curt stared at each other with surprise. They couldn't have been more surprised than I was by the words that had come out of my mouth. I was happy to be in their company and away from my lonely apartment. "When did I so become my father's son?" I thought.

The truth is I was an old student of silence. I had spent so many wordless hours with my father and grandfather, I had forgotten that a nod and the occasional soft laugh didn't pass for much in a group. Years later, Eva would tell me how much it had cost her to be my friend, to work through my silences, the reserve I traded for affection. I wondered if my father, when he sat quietly with me as a child, thought what I thought in that house in Maryland that day. I felt that my feelings for my friends were as plain as the moonlight or as the wind shaking a tree like a pompom.

If it had been for me to choose how to most resemble my father, I would have chosen his durability. He punished his body with heroin for twenty years, not to mention smoking two or more packs of cigarettes a day. When I was nine, he would send me on my bike to the convenience store with five dollars to buy another pack of Winstons. When I was thirty-two and still thought I was a runner, I ran too far and hurt my knee. To this day, I can't run farther than a mile without aggravating it. That injury was the first of many nagging pains waiting for me in the future. Just the other morning after a shower, I toweled myself too vigorously and strained a ligament in my hand. I'm afraid to discover what new levels of fragility wait for me after fifty. For all I know, I'll break a rib every time I sneeze.

If not my father's, I wish I had the durability of at least a mule. I had wanted to be a mule when I was a kid, or at least as smart as one. I envied the intelligence of Francis the Talking Mule whenever I saw his movies on television. He read Einstein for crying out loud. He was worldly, too, as well as brave. I wanted to be all those things.

Each time someone expressed surprise that a "dumb beast" like a mule could talk, Francis would quip, "I hope to kiss a duck I can talk," or, "What trick is there to talking? Any fool can do it." And still I found it painful to talk in class or at home. When other people talked, it was like standing in the rain. All I had to do was watch the sheets of words fall and evaporate.

If you think all mules look alike, you're mistaken. Like humans, some mules are short, fat, or lean. Mix in a blonde, brunette, or even the rare champagne coif, and you have an infinite variety. Imagine James Dean's face with its long, handsome jaw on the stocky body of a Marlon Brando and then add the funny bone of a Rodney Dangerfield, and you have a good picture of Francis.

Whenever I see a pasture with mules or donkeys, I can't help but pull over. At the fence, I click my tongue and call them over. Wary, most will keep eating and ignore me.

If I were a mule in the pasture, I would be the curious one that lopes over to smell the hand of the young man. If he seemed gentle, I would let him stroke one of my soft ears. And if I were feeling brave that day, when he placed his warm hand on my long forehead and the light of my eyes met the light of his, I would try to say everything our lives depended upon.

MUCH IS MADE of people who smile with their eyes. The one-hundred-pound woman everyone in the neighborhood I grew up in knew as Granny didn't have eyes that smiled. They flickered. Her smile grew in the garden where smiles are meant to, her mouth. When her smile spread out like a patch of cactus, I would watch and wait for the magical moment when her face bloomed. She loved to eat prickly pears and would warn us kids to stay away from the ones she grew in the yard. Although I love the taste of nopalitos now, I never did see her eat any of those spiny green pancakes she tended.

Granny lived with her daughter Bertha, along with Bertha's grown sons Richard and David and David's son Anthony, who was a few years younger than me. The back of their mobile home opened up onto a giant deck, where Granny would feed upward of thirty stray cats. Twenty feet past the deck was Jackie's house. Even though Aunt Beulah had raised him, Jackie counted Granny and Bertha, whom he was close to in age, as his real mothers. They had given him the unconditional love he had hungered for.

I sat on the couch while Bertha worked on a crossword puzzle. I can't remember a time when I came over and she wasn't at work on one. Granny too. As I drank from the glass of ice water she handed me, I tried not to spit it out. While manners weren't really talked about in my house, they were important in Granny's. Once I had sat on this same couch eating a candy bar and learned that it was rude to visit someone's house with food and not bring enough to share.

As I took another sip to try and figure out why the water tasted so bitter, I watched Granny return to the kitchen, where she was chopping onions for dinner. I considered complaining about my glass of onion ice water but remembered how Granny's eyes could flare with love one second and then stone the next. I didn't want to chance it, no matter how much I hated the water.

Once, when I had said I hated something, she gently gripped my arm, locked my eyes, and said, "You can't claim to love God and hate something at the same time. Do you love God?"

I wasn't sure at the time if I still did. What I did know was that the correct reply was *Yes*. After I affirmed that I loved God, Granny told me that even though people don't want to admit it, the heart has its limits. It was a relief to know your heart could turn away too much love or disappointment when it came knocking, to say, *Sorry, we're all stocked up. Have a nice day.*

As I sat in their living room with my onion ice water, I thought about this. The summer blazed outside. The curtains, which were drawn on the open windows, hardly moved. There was no breeze that day from the Gulf, or anywhere else. I wanted to leave and find a fan, but I also didn't. Since my grandparents had passed away, Granny had become even more precious to me. When I bent to hug her, I would rest my cheek against her soft, white-gray hair. It was a pillow against which I could have lain and happily passed out of the world.

A DECADE LATER, my mom told Bertha and Granny how I had seen someone walking in Austin who I thought looked like Jackie. My mom said, "You don't think Tomás would have kept going if he thought it was Jackie, do you?"

"No. My baby wouldn't do that," Granny had said, shaking her head.

But hadn't I done that? Hadn't I seen someone who looked like the man I said I loved more than my father and kept driving as my heart pounded? The truth is I didn't want it to be him, because if it was, then he had lost a lot of weight and was doing drugs again. It had to be someone else.

WHEN GRANNY WAS dying in the hospital, she no longer remembered who I was. I sat and listened to her tell me a story I had heard many times.

When she was a young girl, she had ridden her black horse Frank to school. One day, a train conductor working on his engine had seen her standing on Frank's back when she thought no one was around. When she came home from school, she was in trouble.

Granny didn't remember me. I was a kind stranger who had stopped to visit and hear her favorite story and nothing more. I wondered if Jackie would still know me if I saw him on the streets of Austin and stopped to talk to him. Would he still remember all the days that drifted away with the two of us bent over a chessboard, the hours we spent following Kane from one wilderness to another on *Kung Fu*?

I thought maybe I hadn't mattered to Granny. After all, I was just the quiet kid who lived across the street, not one of her own.

Looking at her wrinkled hands, I imagined them when they were soft and young, when the skin of her fingers was as firm as the reins she used to guide Frank. Imagining young Granny bouncing on Frank's back down an almost empty Texas road, I realized that she hadn't forgotten me because she didn't love me. Frank was always destined to be one of her last memories at the end of her life, because he had lived in her mind for over half a century, while she had only known me for a fraction of that.

If I'm lucky enough to live as long as Granny and have time chip away at my already bad memory, I wonder what my Frank will be. When I'm lying lost in a room surrounded by unfamiliar faces, will I still remember Jackie or Granny or my father? Maybe the only story I'll have left is one about a tree I used to climb and how from high in its branches, I could see every part of the world I longed to forget.

BY 2000 I HAD dropped out of my PhD program at Johns Hopkins University. While I still wanted to be a professor one day, my heart wasn't in Hispanic and Italian studies anymore. I had a handful of friends and a master's degree to show for it. During my time in that program, I had my first migraine and episode of vertigo. I was in the computer room where my fellow TAS and I gathered to have lunch and use the computers. One of the TAS filled the room with the aroma of her meatball sub. When I asked her where she had bought it, she said she had made it at home and asked if I wanted a bite. One bite and I told her it was the best meatball sandwich I had ever tasted. A few minutes later, when I was back at the computer, the screen began to slowly circle in front of me like a Ferris wheel. I gripped the table and said to the room that I felt like I was going to fall out of my chair. Two friends steadied me, while another TA called campus security to take me to the health center. I told them I needed to see a doctor right away, but I didn't know for what. My friends steadied me through the hall and then down the stairs like human crutches to the golf cart waiting outside. During the ride to the health center, the left side of my forehead felt like it was being split open. Years later, the vein on that side of my forehead would be so engorged with blood that the skin along it would actually break and bleed. I told the doctor my symptoms, and he said, "Son, I think you've just described your first migraine."

For years, I blamed the migraine and the vertigo on some ingredient in that meatball sandwich. But what I left out when I told that story to friends was how I had been depressed for a year, how my compulsions that I didn't know were compulsions were taking over more and more of my life. During that time, I would do things I hadn't done before, or since, like stare at the forks and knives that were pointing at me when my friends set them down in between bites. I felt assaulted by the invisible lines that extended from the ends of utensils when they were pointed at me. I would shift in my seat to avoid them. Or I would wait until the person wasn't looking and then adjust them quickly. I didn't talk about any of this, or about the depression that had led me to stand under the shower, arms crossed, so the hot water could pool in my arms and feel like someone touching me. Or the times I kept picking up the phone to call my grandmother, only to remember as I was dialing her number that she had passed away six years earlier. And then there was my obsession about missing a call from my mother, which caused me to constantly lift the phone to listen for the dial tone and then quickly hang it back up out of fear that she might be calling at that exact second.

That summer, my then wife and I packed our things and returned to central Texas, where I enrolled in a graduate program in creative writing. In a year, my marriage crumbling because I had refused to admit that something was wrong, I would finally seek help. I had lost interest in almost everything I loved to do. I was withdrawn and felt like someone stumbling around in a fog. My first therapist suggested I meet with a doctor. I was in and out of the doctor's office in about ten minutes. He was in his forties, as I am now, and sat on a stool that swiveled. I walked out of his office with the depression diagnosis I had expected, as well as some news that surprised me. He said I also had obsessive-compulsive disorder. I knew so little about OCD that I was convinced he had to be mistaken. I had never washed my hands hundreds of times a day because I was obsessed with germs like the people I had seen on TV. The doctor was kind and confident, so I trusted him. In my hand I held a prescription for Zoloft, a pill he said would give me a chance to get my depression and OCD under control.

I told very few of my classmates about any of this, because I was afraid people would think I was "crazy," which is what most of us would've thought in Mathis. During all my years growing up in South Texas, I can't even recall knowing a single person who saw a therapist. Prayer and willpower are probably how I would've been told to deal with depression and OCD had I been diagnosed as a kid. Therapists and medication are for rich people was what most of us thought in the South Texas of the eighties and nineties.

AS AN INSTRUCTOR'S assistant in my new graduate program at Texas State University, I shared an office with ten others. When we weren't focused on trying to be better writers, we filled our days with grading mountains of blue book exams. Stacks of two hundred to four hundred per class were not unusual.

While our office was small, we each had a desk. I preferred a desk in the corner. They were anchored in a way that others weren't. Those desks gave you a wall beside you and another ahead of you to at least create the illusion of privacy. A corner desk was like a half closet. I counted myself lucky to have snagged one on the first day of the semester.

In order to make the space a little more my own, I decided to put up pictures. At home it didn't take me long to realize I didn't really have any pictures. We didn't have a camera when I was growing up. Actually, that's not true. We did have one. It was an old Polaroid with giant flashcubes lined along the top. It lasted maybe a month before my father pawned it because his paycheck was gone and he had already gone through my mom's.

If something we owned could be sold and my father could lift it, our family Rumpelstiltskin would transform it into cash and then dope, with the help of the local pawnshops. And when they wouldn't bite, he would find a friend who would. Cameras, tools, jewelry, electronics were all fair game.

My mom once made the mistake of letting my aunt store her freezer in our house while she moved. It was the size of a refrigerator but sat horizontally. My mom and aunt correctly assumed it was too large for my father to move it by himself. I don't think it even lasted a week. Neither my aunt nor mom had factored in the willingness of most addicts to share.

While my father preferred not to share his needles or drugs, he could sell the freezer for so much money that he could easily split a bit of his score with whoever helped him move it.

While my mom and I were at school, he and his friends moved on that bulky freezer like happy crocodiles on a wounded hippo, knowing that there would be plenty to go around.

Since I didn't have any photos to put up in my new shared office, I decided to hang some art over my desk instead. Since I couldn't afford any, I printed a color copy of a painting I couldn't get out of my mind: *Saturn Devouring His Son*.

In Goya's painting, Saturn, the god of time, eats his infant children because it had been prophesied that one of them would revolt against him, just as he had against his father. In a much earlier sketch of this scene, Goya draws Saturn eating one of his children while it gropes at what could be blankets while his leg up to the hip has already disappeared into his father's mouth. The old god looks like he's having a midnight snack in bed. In his left hand, Saturn holds another child tightly by the leg. The outline of this child resembles a chicken thigh with the drumstick still attached.

I found this funny, as I'm sure Goya did as well. Comparing infanticide with a cookout was just the kind of dark humor I loved.

The difference between the sketch and the painting is that in the sketch you identify with the poor children because you can see the face of one of them while the other one joins its hands together as if in prayer. In the painting, the body is headless, and we only see the back of the torso raised to Saturn's mouth. The focus of the painting is Saturn, not his children. The black humor is gone, and we are given instead a father who looks helpless and driven by fear. At its heart, the painting is about one father's desperate struggle to survive.

When I hung my photocopy of this painting above my desk, I felt like it was a portrait of my father and me. The only difference is that unlike in the myth, I crawled into my father's mouth. Every time he shook with fear that this would be the night he would die from withdrawals, I left my bed and helped nurse him, not because I had to, but because I wanted to. I could have pretended not to hear his groans, the way, years later, I would pretend not to hear my mom's boyfriend beat her on the other side of my bedroom wall. Instead, I let my father swallow my childhood one bite at a time. By the time I was eleven and he left our family for good, I felt there was nothing left of my childhood for anyone to consume.

I didn't know how wrong I was.

The photocopy of *Saturn Devouring His Son* lasted on my tiny bit of office wall for only a few weeks. Some of my officemates, as well as a few students, had said it was disgusting. I never found out who tossed it in the trash when I wasn't around. When I couldn't find it behind or under my desk, I felt transported back to Mathis. Here was that old familiar shame again, the encouragement to keep my family, and its problems, out of sight.

Years later my oldest half brother gave me a photo of our father taken around the time when he would have been living with my mom. In the center my father stands, impossibly skinny from drugs, skinnier than I ever remembered him. His pants barely hang onto his hips.

He looms like a wraith in the photo.

He does not look like the strong, muscular version of himself I have carried around in my memory for decades. His black wavy hair, like mine, is long and unkempt, and his sideburns are grown out. His arms drape over the shoulders of my two oldest half brothers in such a way that each of his large hands comes to rest over their chests. His vacant eyes stab through the camera, the photographer, and out beyond to some other place.

There is no question he owns these teenage boys like trophies.

This photo haunts me. And yet, for some reason, I carry it on my phone and can't bring myself to delete it. When I tell stories about my father, I will show people this picture in the way someone that survived an attack from a mountain lion or anaconda might whip out a photo and say, "Check it out. This is what almost ate me!"

I always feel a little shame in these moments. I'd rather show them the Saturn that hung on my office wall. He's so hungry for life. How could anyone not be proud of a father like that?

HOW OFTEN HAD I called my father "the statue at home" or said, "His face was like stone"? And each time, the friend who listened to me would nod and say something about the silence of fathers.

But it's not true—he wasn't all silence. I remember the current of his voice when he would talk to grown-ups, when he would be laughing with his friends, while I, his child, was stuck next to a woman whose face I can never remember. Sometimes she's in her forties. Eyes red. Her hair is often brown, like wood chips or railroad rails or the stitches of a boot sole, like a leather belt, a fake leather belt, like the spears of wheat on a penny. Sometimes it is black or blonde or red. It is hardly ever gray, though.

She is tall and short and plump, but mostly skinny, mostly white. She smells like rain. I hate the rain. It sounds lonelier than I do.

Whether I'm in the back of a car or on a couch or at her kitchen table, she always looks at me the same way. With love and regret. This is the way I wish my father would look at me in the rearview mirror when I catch his eyes. This is the way he never looks at me.

Sometimes she taps her cigarette, and sometimes she even smiles before she whispers a confession about her kids, how old they are, how they're living with her parents until she gets straight. She smells like rain, and I want to be alone. I don't want to remind her of her son who likes to read, who is growing so fast she doesn't believe it, who sighs more and more when she visits.

She wants to muss my hair. Sometimes she does. This makes me want to sigh, but I don't, because I don't like it when my father looks at me and sighs. I loved my mom, but I was in love with my father. Or the idea of him. I was head over heels for the man I wanted him to be. I can see it now. It was so obvious.

"Mas claro no canta un gallo," my grandfather would have said. And he would have been right too. Time and again, there is my father teaching us that a heart doesn't stop when you crack a person's chest open. If anything, it beats faster. And harder.

Why can't I ever find my mom in these memories? She must be the couch I sit on or the flickering lamp on the table beside the women who wish I was their son or daughter because if I were, then I would be with them, and the happiness that is swallowing them would feel a little more like warm raindrops and a little less like water racing down the street.

In these moments, my father's laugh was the one thing that could break the spell of my discomfort. To watch television with him was to be open to the rupture of his laughter. When he heard something truly funny, sound would explode from his reserved, still face. To witness it was jarring, but even more so if you had your back to him.

I didn't know my laugh was his laugh until I was nearly forty, about to be divorced, and decided I no longer needed to muffle my laugh out of consideration for others.

Before this moment, people would have probably described my laugh as close to the low bubble of boiling water. And I wouldn't have disagreed. Then I started relaxing my arm every time it shot up to my mouth when one of my laughs was about to escape. It would be a year before my arm would lie calmly by my side while I laughed. Every now and then, I will feel the slightest of twitches from my arm. Somewhere deep inside my shoulder, a memory locked into my ligaments awakens and remembers its old job to try and rescue me from the judgment and displeasure of others.

That summer at a writer's conference, while celebrating life, words, old and new friends, I stopped apologizing when air rushed out of my lungs and laughed as loud and as long as my body wanted. If I was inside a building, my laugh would happily bounce from wall to wall and fill the space for a few seconds. People whipped their heads around, stared, registered my body's joy, and then smiled. The absence of scowls was the first thing I didn't expect. The second was how much I sounded like my father.

All of a sudden, my father was with me, our laugh echoing across the green fields in one of my favorite places in the world. I hadn't planned to find him in Vermont, and yet, there he was, waiting patiently inside my chest all this time.

In the barn where everyone caught their breath with a snack and a drink, he was in the rafters. By the fireplace in the inn, he rushed past the flames and up the chimney. I told one of my new friends that I was done with sadness, that I was a Joy Man now.

One afternoon, as the sun pulled its gold hand from the face of a green field, a moose appeared in the distance. She was the color of mud before it dries. Her ears were long as knives, and she had the legs of a dancer.

Everyone crowded the edge of the porch to see her. She stared at us for a long minute, huffed, and then ran in a circle. When she disappeared into the tall trees, I heard the forest break against her body like it had always done.

WHO KNOWS HOW a runner's mind works. They say that when Pheidippides ran from Marathon to Athens with news of victory over the Persians, he said, "Joy to you, we've won!"

Then he fell down dead.

This sounds like a cautionary tale, not an inspirational one.

Maybe runner's high is what pulls runners back to the road day after day. In ten years of running, I never felt it. Not once.

Neuroscientists say the brain floods with endorphins during a runner's high. The parts of the brain that turn wet and swampy with endorphins from a runner's high are the same parts that light up when we fall in love.

The formula sounds simple: run far enough and you'll feel like you've just sunk deep into the arms of the love of your life. I pounded the road for a decade looking for that love and then for something else.

CAN BONES SHAKE? A friend remembered the other day that inside she's a skeleton. When it felt like a knife was under my ribs around mile one, was that the period of the first sentence in a tragedy or a comedy? And how would I know the difference?

"When one thing looks like another, details matter," I told the guy who thought an albatross and a seagull were the same.

An albatross can fly for hours without ever landing. What's more, it does this without discomfort, because evolution has made it possible for the albatross to keep its wings extended without strain on its muscles. If we were meant to run long distances, then we would arrive out of the womb able to glide down the road for hours on end.

The cheetah gets all the press for being the fastest land mammal, at seventy miles per hour. Usain Bolt from Jamaica topped out at twenty-seven miles per hour. Even if he, our fastest human, could maintain this speed for longer than ten seconds, he'd still be slower than the pronghorn antelope that runs an easy pace of thirty miles per hour for twenty miles. The world record for the marathon is two hours and three minutes. A pronghorn could cover this distance in forty-five minutes. Not because of training, but because it was born to do so.

Visit the finish line of any long-distance race, with its mix of misery and glee, and the truth is obvious: a human is no albatross or pronghorn.

BECAUSE OUR BODIES are being tortured during a long run, runner's high is a way to cope. While running away from the hungry bear at your door or the hockey mask–wearing serial killer is a perfectly natural act, you don't need to run twenty-six miles to get away. If they haven't caught you after the first mile, chances are you're safe and can stop.

When I ran cross-country in high school, our coach would ask us to run along the frontage road of i-37 toward Corpus Christi until we reached a group of telephone poles named Three Pole. To Three Pole and back was about three miles. One day, I felt strong and told a teammate that I was going to push past Three

Pole until I had run the giant, rectangular block our high school had been built on.

Nine miles later, as my high school appeared in the distance, the muscles in my legs felt like firewood, stiff and itchy. I had chased a runner's high but didn't find it. Endorphins never drenched my brain to make me fall in love with the strike of my feet against the road that had to end where I started, a road that didn't lead me, even for a few brief minutes, in a chemical fog, away from my life. If I couldn't feel worthy of real love, then why not fake love? Maybe fake love was waiting for me at mile ten with a goofy grin. Hadn't I pounded my bones on the road enough to fall in love with the very punishment I had chosen?

THE SEAGULL IS small compared to the albatross. It can't soar into the air and leave the world behind for hours and hours. It will scrap and fight and plot for what it wants, what it needs.

A seagull once tried to follow me into a restaurant in Port Townsend, Washington. I ordered a slice of pizza and then took a seat at the window and watched it. We stared at each other through the glass. We both wanted the same thing. When a father holding his little daughter's hand approached the door, the gull walked off. I was stunned his pink feet were enough. He must have been saving his wings for other things.

YOU COULDN'T MISS the jersey if you needed glasses. Gold with maroon trim. A giant twenty-three under the word CAVS. Last year the kid wore a Heat jersey to the courts. This year his favorite player, LeBron James, is back in Ohio.

Cleveland is 1,243 miles north of Miami. If the Rust Belt were a real belt, Cleveland would be the cracked red spot in the center of its buckle. One city has sand, the other grit. One Celia Cruz, the other Dwight Yoakum. Both have had their hearts broken by number twenty-three. Except for this kid, who is from neither place, who follows not teams but the man.

So deep is the kid's devotion that I saw him hit a three pointer, walk to the other end of the court, and raise one knee, then the other, all while pushing the invisible earth he had just razed back down with his hands. The celebration of his shooting prowess ended with him pounding his chest just like LeBron, the love of his young life.

Sometimes I think, *What a sad bastard*, and then other times, I'm envious that he can still experience a love so naive and pure as to make him impervious to the ridicule of all the guys on the sideline. And at twenty years of age, no less. Usually that kind of idolatry, especially male on male, is stomped on, jeered at, and shamed out of a young boy much sooner.

During the nineties I was infatuated with Michael Jordan (may the Celtic gods forgive me) when Boston languished and spent the playoffs sitting at home. My tongue wagging every time I drove to the basket, I was trying to fulfill the wet dream of some Gatorade executive and "be like Mike." But jokes behind my back, to my face, all the usual tactics of intimidation and shame that boys are masters at, cured me of this fixation, and I relented and began just being me on the court. That and almost biting my tongue in half while trying to do a reverse layup did the trick.

But this kid with the thin moustache and the floppy hair (he should've picked Pistol Pete) is still at it. What a piece of luck for him to be already a young man in college and not yet have been broken on the rack of male shame.

That I call him a kid reveals a sad fact. I'm old. Or at least old enough to be this kid's father. I call him a kid, for Christ's sake. Living in a college town used to make me feel young, but now that I'm the same age of the parents of my students, a polite "sir" or "mister" waits around every corner for me.

One day, I woke up and became one of the old guys I played ball with growing up, only without a cool nickname, like Joe Dog (animal control officer) or Gator (ladies' man), the Mexican Magic Johnson of Mathis, Texas. Secretly, I dream that one day I'll play a game with a former student and after he calls me professor, the other kids will pick up on it so that before I know it, I'll be able to step on any court in San Marcos and be known as the Professor. But who am I kidding, what could I possibly teach that they couldn't learn from playing one on one with one of their parents? Old equals slow. Surely they can learn that anywhere.

It's been at least six or seven years since I gave up defending guards. No longer can I lock down the opposing team's shooting guards and make them reluctant passers. Where my defense used to be smothering, now it's like a stick of butter on a sidewalk in summer. I'm like the plastic chair the coaches used during practice for us to shoot over and dribble around.

Because I'm also just as slow on offense, now I play inside with the bigs, with the guys who at twenty have all the quickness of a thirty-nine-year-old. Sad bastards.

Their existence reminds me that things could have been worse. I need to find some guys my own age to run with, men for whom time has slowed down just as much, so that maybe I can move back out to the wing. I never saw my father or grandfather play basketball. Any sport, really. Maybe they were too old. I once heard that my father had been a good runner, the fastest in his school. Then he moved to another school, and when he realized the Black kids were as fast or faster than he was, he started chasing girls and beer instead.

Whenever my eyebrows dip and perch like a bird with black wings in the center of my face and my mind feels thick with fog and everything from a yellow light turning red too fast to a drop of rain makes me sad, I grab my ball and find the nearest court.

One game of around the world and back is enough to set my spirit straight. For years now, seeing the ball go through that metal circle has made my spinning world slow and, in slowing, peaceful and harmless again. And if on an outdoor court, so much the better. The kind Jackie and I played on once when I was thirteen, or maybe fourteen, and we were on the same team. He was winded because it was full court and because he smoked and was thirty-five and never exercised. It seemed like his every shot found the bottom of the net, though. Bank, fall away, layup, corner three, all as perfect as when we won and he put his tired arm around my shoulder.

I wanted people to mistake me for his son the way they did when we were out of town, to forget that he was Black and I was Mexican and that we looked nothing alike. But this was Mathis, and it was home, where everyone knew his real son and my real father.

But the kid, I'm forgetting about the kid.

He's a couple of inches taller than I am, but chubby. By all rights, he should play down low, but at some point in his life, he probably watched a seven-footer like Dirk Nowitzki sink a three-point shot and found his calling on the court. And boy, can he shoot. Before my team took the court to play his winning team, I watched him sink three after three. His defenders would get closer, and he'd push his set shot farther and farther behind the arc, accepting the challenge of their dares as he swished one after another.

When it was my team's turn to play, I drew the assignment to guard him. Determined not to let him destroy our chances of winning with his outside shooting, not to mention denying him an opportunity to emulate LeBron's celebration, I held him scoreless with a simple defensive strategy that played to my speed: I stood next to him. The whole game. The few times he had the ball, he passed it away on account of his not liking to dribble and his inability to shoot while I was standing there. A few minutes in, I could tell my defense made him mad.

Every time I put my hand in his face and denied him a shot, he glared. When I followed him around closely, not letting anyone pass him the ball, he huffed. He even tried to rough me up with a forearm to my chest. I probably shouldn't admit to playing rough with kids, but I couldn't pass up his invitation, so I gave him a hard shove. And that's when it happened. Finger jammed.

Turned out, his chubby body wasn't quite as soft as it appeared. I might as well have jabbed my index finger at a bag of cement. That was three weeks ago, and while my finger is getting better, I still can't shoot without pain. So I've done the only thing left to do, learn to shoot with my left.

For a long time now, my favorite spot has been the city park. Situated between a spring-fed river and railroad tracks, I don't need headphones to pipe in music, because the sound of a train rumbling by and kids on tubes laughing and drinking beer, who don't yet know how much the world will mistreat them, are a good and proper soundtrack to my life. Not to mention the male grackles who are in heat and puffed up to twice their size and doing their little circle dance and piping their sharp squeaks into the air in the hope of getting laid. Sometimes, this is all I need for a day to feel like a win.

On the green court, with its white lines, I put up shot after shot, badly missing, not even getting the benefit of a gentle roll that my right hand brought me. And then one went in. But now I was farther away as I circled the world. And for another to go in, I'd have to be perfect. Perfect spin, perfect angle, and perfect height, so that it wouldn't touch the rim. And then I was in my backyard again when I was nine, shooting all day and night at a red milk crate whose bottom I had knocked out, which I had nailed to a tree, along with some rotten plywood for a backboard. That rim wouldn't suffer anything but perfection in order for a shot to go in. Back then, I was like the kid and too dumb to know what bravery was, and so I threw my round ball, arcing up high like Larry Bird's shot, at a square hole and wrestled with the laws of geometry.

An hour later (twice as long as it usually takes me), my globe-trotting done, I went to the corner and took Jackie's favorite shot and wouldn't leave until it went in. I squared my shoulders, bent my knees, and cocked back my arm and flicked my left wrist as I rose and left the ground for a second. *Clank.* That sound over and over. *Clank* for yellow lights. *Clank* for shame. *Clank* for betrayal. *Clank* for pride. *Clank* for the body's sadness. *Clank clank clank* and then, swish. No rim, just a leather globe passing through and snapping the net so that from this spot in the corner, unlike any other spot on the court, when it goes clean through, instead of *swish*, the net says *Jack.* When my right hand is well, I snap that net again and again until the world goes calm, and mute, and all I can hear is *Jack Jack Jack* because everything is right and has stopped burning, except for the fire deep in my shoulder.

ON FRIDAY, NOVEMBER 1, 2013, an old friend from high school tells me Jackie has cancer. She wrote me at 10:53 a.m., but I don't read the message until 11:27 a.m. Every minute feels heavy.

The cancer is late stage. It has found its way into most of his body. Where is he?

Hospice? At home? Is there a phone number? What are the names of his sisters? His brother?

She doesn't have the answers to any of these questions, except one. He's in Austin. In time, she finds out he's gone home to die. Three months is all the time he has left, the doctors say. There is nothing that can be done. By the time she tells me all of this, the information is fourthhand, maybe fifth. A single line of news about him, with the exception of how to find him, makes its way out of Austin, down to San Antonio, then farther south and to the east to Mathis from where she swings it back north to me in San Marcos.

Jackie is in Austin, an hour's drive away from me once I get an address. Thirty-eight miles, give or take.

Any day, I expect to hear good news. The scene that plays through my mind is the same every time: I park outside the house of one of his sisters and take a deep breath. I knock on the door and wait for footsteps, but all I hear are grackles in the trees. It's late, and traffic slowed me down. I wonder how long they'll let me stay to talk with him or how much energy he'll have. If he can only talk for an hour, I'll go have dinner and then come back. Maybe I can bring him back some tacos or soup to eat. Has he ever had Thai food? I've just discovered Thai, and maybe I can introduce him to it. Something vegan would be good too. He doesn't know about that.

Even the dying can eat healthy, right? Or if he needs to rest and falls asleep, maybe I can lay my head next to his arm while he sleeps and close my eyes and remember how he used to look before his hair turned white, as I'm sure his has, when his body was still strong. If I cancel the classes I'm teaching the next day, will his family let me stay the night? There's so much to tell him. It's been seventeen years since I last saw his face or heard his voice. What if he doesn't remember me or does but won't see me? Can I cancel my classes for the week? What will I tell them? Will I tell them my father has cancer and will be dead soon? What does it take to make someone your father? What are the words you have to say, and what do you have to carry in your heart when you say them? What kind of conviction do you need to make a man who has helped raise you, who pushed you out of his life seventeen years ago, into a father? Is there a form to fill out? Does he even have to agree, or can he be your father against his very own will, because he is, and has been, even though he has not laid eyes on you for a time that is longer than all the years you knew each other?

The door before which I stood in my imagination never opened. No one answered it, and as the days turned into weeks, still there was no way to find him. On December 3 my friend became the bearer of bad news for a second time when she reached out to me once more.

Jackie was dead.

Just five days earlier on Thanksgiving Day, he had passed away in Austin. I had been in Austin that day, too, drinking wine and eating dumplings, with new friends who had given me an opportunity to not be alone. As I had looked around the dining room at the food and smiles, the soft light, I had thought, *Happy Thanksgiving, Jack. Happy Thanksgiving.*

THE MONTHS CRAWL by, and it is summer. In Vermont for a friend's wedding, I dropped my line into the Winooski River again and again, and each time I reeled it back in, the same worm was still hanging on. I don't know that the worm could be called persistent, since the worm didn't have any say in the situation or its outcome. As I dunked the worm and then teased it back near the surface, so that it was still beneath the water but close enough to its surface to see the sun and the reflection of the world it would never return to, I thought about my father's love of fishing and the handful of times we'd been and about how although as a child I felt like I was swimming in the waters of his life, I never truly was.

I had been snagged.

So was my mom.

So were his wife and his other children.

He had been a silhouette. He kept us scuttling near the surface as the wide mouths of large and dark things rose from the deep to inspect us and gauge their hunger.

When my worm finally disappeared into the cool brown waters, it was up to me to set the next one just like my friend

Will had shown me before he went back to work, a couple of shiny brown trout hanging wet in his bag. It had probably been twenty years since I had been fishing. And that was surf fishing on Padre Island with my high school girlfriend and her father and brothers. We hauled in dozens of whiting that day. They shone like silver knives in our bucket.

In the light of early evening, all you had to do was wade out to a sandbar and watch the schools of whiting move dark beneath the surface of the water and cast right in the middle to get a hit. When we started out, for bait we used a fish we cut up into chunks. Imagine tempting a creature with the taste of its own kind. I don't know what that says more about—us, who are smart enough to figure out some fish will eat their own, or the fish that is either too cruel or too stupid to know any better.

When I nudged the soft dirt in the container of worms Will had left me, I found a slow fat one that looked just right. As I tried to get a hold of its neck, if a worm can be said to have such a thing, it coiled and flipped in my hand so that I had to drop it and start over. By the time I had it firm and had angled the hook just right so I could thread it along the inside of its body, the worm had done what some worms do and broken off part of its tail. The worm didn't know that I wasn't a robin or warbler that Mother Nature or God or both had spent unnumbered years preparing it to escape from. What it did know was that death was upon it, and if by some chance it was being given a choice between living and dying, it chose living. I picked up its tail and felt the segments with my finger. It wiggled. I couldn't shake the thought that if I were a bird, I would've had a meal and the worm, the worm would have kept its life.

My mom and I coiled and flipped for years, but we always ended up back in the water. My baby brother was too young to know he shouldn't hug the hook, and so he did. When we released our hearts and let my father pull them out, we were finally free. Two wet tiny things between his fingers. By the time his shocked face realized our hearts alone weren't enough, we had crawled away.

Even as I felt pity for the worm on my hook and a sense that what I was doing was wrong, it didn't slow or stop my hand. I just kept going until I had a pink J hanging from the end of my line. The only part of it that I hadn't run through was its head, which moved a little, until I dropped my line back in the river, and then it didn't move anymore after that.

WHEN WORD HAD come that Jackie was gone, I stopped trying to find his family, out of respect for their privacy and grief. Over the next few months, I checked obituaries in the *Austin-American Statesman*, but no luck. I searched all corners of the Internet, including grave-finding websites, but my search came up empty time and again.

I channeled my grief into searching for him, and before long, he was not gone at all, because I could hear him in my mind again. The voice and laugh that had been by my side the entire time we were estranged were still there. I began to forget that he was really gone. The month when a brief window opened up the possibility that I might actually see him and hold his hand and kiss his cheek, tell him about everything that had happened to me since I had last seen him (my marriage, an MFA, my life as a teacher and a writer, my first book, the impending divorce, my new friends), felt more and more like a dream, like a moment in my life when I had imagined that I actually could have talked to him again. For all the pain I had felt, his loss was starting to not feel real.

In the winter of 2014, just as the year was about to turn, my then fiancée told me she had found Jackie's grave. If I had not been back in New England, two thousand miles away at the Vermont College of Fine Arts, I would have driven to the cemetery that day. This was my first time teaching in an MFA program, and while I had been enjoying the experience, had felt reinvigorated as a teacher, it was hard for me to focus. Now that Jackie was found, I should have been happy. But when I tried to talk to him in my mind, there was no response. When I spoke to him, there was only silence instead of one of his favorite replies, like "Ask me no questions, and I'll tell you no lies" or "I see, I see, said the blind man."

When the new year was minutes old, it already rang hollow. I had lost him all over again, and there was nothing I could do about it. Standing next to my friends, I watched the fireworks light up Montpelier and wondered if the sky was exploding over Jackie's grave or if his patch of Texas night was as dark and quiet as my heart.

IT WAS RAINING. I had just finished teaching a class on sentence fragments. The class ended on a tangent. This was not unusual. A student had said, "Women don't need equal pay, because men give us stuff—that evens everything out."

"Stuff? What kind of stuff?" I said.

"I don't know. Like jewelry and a house and cars."

She said this with two minutes left, so I let it go. You need more than two minutes to fix a broken thought like that. Anyhow, I had somewhere to go. Today was the day. In thirty minutes, if the traffic cooperated, I would be in Manor, Texas.

As I slugged through the gray afternoon in rush hour traffic, I finally made my way into East Austin. The whole time, I debated whether to take the toll road or not. I would only save five minutes if I took the toll road. It had been over a year now since I had heard of Jackie's death but seventeen years since I had last seen him. Five minutes made the wait seem longer, so I took the toll road. The speed limit was eighty so I did ninety.

Just as Austin disappeared in my rearview, Manor was upon me. It didn't look like much. I had driven through small towns like this all my life in South Texas. A few turns and I was in cow country. I passed a sign advertising salvation, outside an abandoned church. By the time I reached Wells School Road, my heart thumped like a washing machine out of balance.

When I first found the address and did a little digging, the mystery of why Jackie would be buried outside Austin finally made sense. The Wells School Road cemetery was the overflow indigent cemetery for Travis County. The one in Austin had filled to capacity, so the city bought ninety-five acres in the sticks.

Cemeteries hadn't meant much to me until I saw a homeless man who looked like Jackie. That was when I knew finding his grave wasn't about saying goodbye so much as having proof that he was really gone. What if he was still alive and this was a different Jackie Powell?

The rain had stopped. Or maybe I just drove far enough that I came out from under that gray cloud. Even though the sign said I was in the right place, the abandoned barn off to the side gave me doubts. There were also big tractors for building roads parked next to neat piles of different kinds of dirt and rock. When I saw a few wood crosses in a muddy field, I parked the car.

The county had made three of four large rectangles of dirt with concrete borders. Each rectangle was two coffins wide if the people were laid head to toe. You could probably fit fifty people in each rectangle. Tacked onto the long sides of each border were metal placards with a name, birth and death dates, and the location of that person's grave.

I looked for BLOCK 2, LOT B, SPACE 27.

Then I was there. The birth and death years matched what I knew. His grave startled me. Like many of the other graves, there wasn't enough dirt on Jackie's plot, so in many places, it was sunken. He was down there. I could feel the truth of it. That much was clear now. He was no longer in the street homeless or shaking on someone's couch from withdrawals or lying in bed as cancer chewed his body up.

Relief gave way to tears and a slow growl. The sound in my throat was angry and sickly. I was like a chained-up dog that had been kicked too many times. When I stopped shaking, I sat and let the wet wind blow the afternoon away.

WHEN I RETURNED two months later, my mom and I unloaded ten bags of lava rocks we had bought in the garden department of Lowe's. The sun was out, and it was quickly burning away the dampness inside each bag. While I carried each one over to Jackie's grave and dumped it, my mom spread the rocks around with a shovel. They were the color of old blood.

When we finished, his grave was even and full but still looked empty without a headstone. We walked over to the city's giant pile of limestone rocks, and together we picked one out. It was only about half a football field from the rocks to Jackie's grave, but I needed to stop every ten feet or so to rest, because the rock we had chosen was so heavy.

My mom and I stared at our work quietly. The stone sat lop-sided. It reminded me how anything could be a crown if it sat on the head of a king.

WHEN I WAS a kid, I felt like I could build anything. The two-by-six was like most any other. It had sat in a corner of our backyard in Mathis so long that it no longer had that fresh-cut smell that is the perfume of every lumberyard. When I lifted it from the grass, it left its shape behind, and I couldn't help but wonder if the ants and rolly pollies would resent this yellow break in their forest. Or maybe they would treat it as a park where they would sun with their little ones on vacation? I hit the piece of wood against the house to knock off the dirt. When I ran it under water, it turned the color of the bran flakes my mom always bought us. I knew it would make a perfect Thor's hammer.

To say my brother and I were obsessed with weapons is a stretch. After all, by the time he was ten years old, my little brother owned at least a dozen knives. His collection contained different sizes and different blades. Among them there was a pen knife, a dagger, a machete, and his pride and joy, a survival knife with a compass built into the handle. Someone had sold it to him when he was nine at the flea market in town. It was a weapon worthy of Rambo himself, a movie we watched all the time. My little brother had seen some things in his first decade of life, so who could blame him for wanting to be prepared, especially if Toro came back.

With the exception of the blowgun he bought at Merle Norman, most of the weapons my brother liked required being close to your target. Sure, you can throw a knife, but if you miss, then that knife becomes a weapon that can be used against you. I wanted a weapon that could be thrown, make contact, and then return to my hand, like Thor's hammer, Mjölnir, did in the comic books. As it flew away from his hand and pulverized frost giants and all sorts of monsters, he only had to open his hand to make it reverse course and return to him. What could be more perfect?

IT WAS THE last few days of December 2017, and I was back at wintry Vermont College, teaching. That night, I had the pleasure of introducing Tyehimba Jess before he shared his poetry with us. With his syncopated sonnets about Millie and Christine McKoy, conjoined twins born into slavery in the American South, he took the audience on a journey exploring the limits of suffering and love, of one body singing two songs. I was in a daze when his powerful presentation ended. Before I left the chapel, where the reading had taken place, to join the reception for Tyehimba, I checked my phone for messages. There was a text message from my mother.

Your dad is in hospital
Gigi wants to talk to you.

Who is Gigi?

Gigolo Joe jr

Oooooh. What's his phone number? Did you give him
   my number?

Yes

I just got his voicemail just now. I'll call him in a few
   minutes.

When I was a kid, everyone in Mathis called my oldest half brother Jiggy (his given name was Joe Jr.), because he liked to date older women. It had been over a decade since I had heard that name and even longer since we had spoken, and now here I was with his voicemail waiting on my phone. I told someone I needed to make a phone call and slipped into an empty classroom.

It was 7:30 p.m. I walked over to the dark windows and held my hand over the radiator. The ground was covered in snow outside. The winter storm that had dropped two inches of snow on central Texas on December 7 had moved east and pounded the South. In the days that followed, it crawled up the Atlantic coast and now had New England in its sights. I couldn't outrun it any more than I could the news that waited in the voicemail.

When the voicemail ended after a long thirty-five seconds, some of his words spun through my mind like a dog chasing its own tail: "This is your brother . . . Christus Spohn . . . stage 4 cancer . . . call me back."

I stared out the window. The night was quiet, and with the reading over, the building had emptied. The radiator whispered.

My brother Joe reminded me that this was not the first time our father had been diagnosed with lung cancer. Fifteen years before, doctors had removed half a lung to stem the spread of the cancer. He had also been diagnosed with asbestosis at that time, a result of exposure from all the years when he worked construction. After his initial diagnosis, a decade and a half prior, our father kept smoking. And so, of course, here we were. The lung cancer was stage 4. It had metastasized to his kidney, liver, and brain. In the months to come, I would type those last two sentences so often that I started copying and pasting them into new text messages to friends that I hadn't reached out to yet.

When I called the number Joe had given me to Christus Spohn, the hospital where my father was, I expected the switchboard operator to answer. Instead, my father did. When I heard his voice, I was glad that I had pulled a chair up to the window and sat down. His voice was like an arrow cutting through the air. While I strained to hear him, the joy in his voice when he realized it was me was clear. It stung hard.

He had missed me. I was stunned.

When I told him that I was so sorry to hear that he was sick and in the hospital, he simply said, "It happens." I can't count the number of times that in the exact same way I've brushed off the concern of people who cared about me.

After I told him how I was, I found myself saying what I would have found unsayable only minutes before: "I'm out of state right now, but when I get back to Texas, I'll come see you." He said how happy he was to hear my voice and that he couldn't wait to see me. I hung up and struggled to recognize the face with tears staring at me from the window. Whom was I becoming?

When I woke the next morning, I realized that the last time we had spoken was after his first cancer diagnosis. He had said then that if I wanted a relationship with him that I should make an effort to visit and spend time with him. I had answered him with silence year after year as I waited for the call that he had passed, a call that never came. Back then, I had thought Jackie had already been the dad I needed and that I didn't need a dad anymore. And since my father and I had so little in common, what was the point of trying to be friends? I reasoned that I had enough friends in my life that I would be okay without one more. And so I let the years slip by in silence.

It was 6:00 a.m., and I couldn't go back to sleep. Outside, a single bird sang to the snowy morning. A few minutes of research on my phone told me it was a hermit thrush. I couldn't help but think of my favorite hermit thrush in all of poetry, the one in Walt Whitman's "When Lilacs Last in the Dooryard Bloom'd." In this elegy for the recently assassinated President Lincoln, it is the thrush that announces death; it provides the music to celebrate the arrival of "lovely and soothing death." But it takes time for the speaker in Whitman's poem to realize this, having first mistaken the thrush's song as a sad song. Whitman writes,

> Sing on, sing on you gray-brown bird,
> Sing from the swamps, the recesses, pour your chant
>   from the bushes,
> Limitless out of the dusk, out of the cedars and pines.
>
> Sing on dearest brother, warble your reedy song,
> Loud human song, with voice of uttermost woe.

Hermit thrushes from Vermont usually migrate south during the winter. A few stay behind. Even when the temperatures dropped to twenty below zero, this little bird sat in the tree outside my window and kept filling my room with song.

I SAWED THE two-by-six into a rectangle. Then I marked and cut the ends to make it an octagon. For a handle, I nailed a round chair leg to the center of the head of my hammer. I wrapped the handle in duct tape in order to keep the nails from further splitting the wood. I practiced throwing it underhanded like Thor so often did in the comic books. I hit trees, the walls of our house, a fence. But each time I struck something, I had to walk over to pick the hammer up. For a while I used a thin rope attached to the handle to pull the hammer back to me. I tied the other end of the rope to my wrist. But it felt ridiculous. And what's worse, if someone picked up the hammer before I could pull it back to me, then it would be me they had at the end of the rope.

In time, I replaced Thor's hammer with a sling shot, a crossbow, and a boomerang. I was twelve and "the man of the house" now. But I didn't have the strength of a man. I had seen a man try to kill my mother. If that man, or another man like him, wanted to lay his hands on me, he could easily kill me. Kill me, my brother, and my mother. He could kill us all.

ONE JANUARY MORNING, a few days after returning to Texas from Vermont, my brother and I pulled up to my father's house in Mathis. This was the home where he and his wife had raised their children.

Would I be made to feel welcome?

Would his wife ignore me?

Did she hate me?

All these questions ran through my head as we walked up. I was surprised when my brother opened the door without knocking and entered. In the dark living room, the stone fireplace my father had built sat. A Volkswagen Beetle was hardly bigger. It was as if a giant had set his hat on the ground one day, and by the time he remembered to put it back on, someone had built a house around it.

We met my father's wife. Her face looked soft as a sand dollar. I said "Mucho gusto," and nodded, as we moved to the bedroom. When my father saw us, he sat up and smiled. The last time I had seen him, he was fifty-two and I was twenty-three. Now here we were at seventy and forty-one.

The distance I walked to hug him was three steps. Within those steps was an eighteen-year desert. On the ground were the skeletons of people we'd never see again. The land was bitter and salted, because there had once been an ocean in its place, an ocean we would never swim in again.

Holding him in my arms, we cried.

"I missed you, mijo."

I could only nod. When he sat up on the edge of the bed, I rubbed his back and stroked his hair. I was confused by the way I was comforting him. It felt so natural I didn't have to think about it, like shooting a basketball. Buried deep in the muscles of my body was the memory of how to comfort him, because I had done it so many times as a tired child, a child who wanted nothing more than to go back to sleep. There are some things the body never forgets.

"Don't cry, mijo. Everyone's number gets called eventually. I ain't afraid to go; it's just the suffering I don't like."

I thought, *Yeah, going is what you've always been good at, going into drugs and leaving us waiting for days and days. Suffering isn't what you're good at—it's what you made me good at . . .*

His purple Do Not Resuscitate bracelet caught my eye long enough for me to notice his hand in my hand and that although we have the same long fingers, I have the thumbnails of my mom's mom. Then I noticed we have different hairlines. And with all the weight he'd lost, his face was like a bird's now, while mine was like a pumpkin.

"Have you gotten taller, mijo?"

"No, still five feet ten. Except for the days I feel taller."

He laughed, and then my six-foot-three little brother sitting on the other side of my father said, "Except for when you're standing next to me." After our laughter stopped shaking the bed, he said, "Did you get married?"

"Yeah, but I got divorced."

"Any kids?"

"No, no kids."

He nodded and said, "A friend was telling me the other day how much he had to pay in child support. He said sometimes it's just cheaper to keep them!" His weak body burst in a laugh that I knew as my own.

ACCORDING TO *Encyclopedia Britannica*, there are two types of boomerangs. The returning boomerang is light and one to two feet long and was used in Australia mostly as a toy or in tournaments. My knowledge of boomerangs came from what I saw on television, and thus as a kid, I thought the returning kind was the only kind there was. And because I was a child, it never dawned on me that a crescent-shaped stick could not in reality strike someone and then return to my hand. On the other hand, it describes the nonreturning boomerang as "longer, straighter, and heavier than the returning variety. With it animals were maimed and killed, while in warfare it caused serious injuries and death." Unlike the Aboriginals, I never carved anything on my boomerang. I wanted to be safe, and so I didn't care what the boomerang looked like.

I practiced throwing it all day. I tried to wrap it around a tree. A fencepost. The wire my mom hung our clothes on. Each time I struck the tree, its bark broke off. My boomerang nicked the fencepost until the wood turned soft. It wrapped around the clothes wire and looped to the ground. I felt like a failure, even as my boomerang did exactly what I had made it to do.

TWO WEEKS LATER I was back in Mathis for a BBQ benefit my family organized. My father didn't have any life insurance, so all the proceeds would help pay for his final expenses. My brother Joe cooked more chicken quarters than I could count. Someone made potato salad, someone else beans. There were desserts and Valentine's Day baskets to raffle.

I didn't expect my father to show up to his own benefit, but there he was, looking as sharp as he ever had. My brother and I pulled up to the auto parts store that had let my family use their parking lot. The first thing I noticed was my father's silver pencil-thin mustache with handlebars. It was immaculate. He wore a black button-down shirt with charcoal stripes over a white undershirt, and his slacks were the color of an old penny. That one leg bunched over the top of his shiny maroon alligator boots did not diminish how regal he looked. A black fedora with a cream feather in the band and a tan suede jacket with the longest wool collar I'd ever seen kept the drizzle off him. He was cold. And thin.

Since I had last seen him, he had decided not to undergo treatment and instead do home hospice. That afternoon at the benefit, I met his sister Mary. And her daughters, who, even though I was meeting them for the first time, welcomed me with open arms. I was slowly beginning to feel less like an outsider in my father's family. As I stared at the slices of cake in their plastic boxes, I heard Ramon la Copa's voice behind me say, "Move aside, *Two and a Half Men*! Don't hog all the sugar, Charlie Sheen."

For as long as I could remember, Ramon would walk the streets of Mathis, giant fountain drink in hand, and chat with anyone who would listen. He always seemed to be at every sporting event, cheering on the home team. He also gave everyone a nickname. In high school when he saw my friend Marlo, he'd say, "Hey, Jessie from *Saved by the Bell*!" Decades after my friend Isaac graduated from high school and started shaving his head and hitting the gym, he became Stone Cold Steve Austin. As I smiled and stepped aside for Ramon, I thought about how Mathis has no greater way to welcome you back than to give you a new name.

The next day, I began my drive back to central Texas. It was a Sunday morning, and instead of taking the interstate through San Antonio, I took the back roads. I hadn't gone twenty miles when a black car with tinted windows merged into the empty lane beside me. His driving was erratic, and so I sped past him. A few seconds after I passed him, I looked in the rearview mirror and saw that he was driving down the stripe dividing the two lanes. He was coming up on me fast and was about to slam into the back of my car. I jerked onto the shoulder and slammed on my brakes. As he flew past me, my car began to spin back into the road. I didn't know how to stop my car from spinning across the road and into the median, which I knew would flip me in the air. Not knowing what to do, I did the only thing I could think of and took my foot off the brake. The spin stopped almost immediately. My car was left sitting across both lanes, and by some miracle, there wasn't another car in sight. Somehow the car had shifted into neutral. I took a deep breath, put it in drive, and parked on the shoulder. The black car was gone, and in less than a minute, the road was busy again with cars.

No one had witnessed anything. Not the black car, not the spinning. I called my mom and told her how I had almost beat my father into the grave. She didn't find my joke as funny as I did.

Three weeks later I would see my father alive for the last time. His home was filled with his family and friends. I sat by his bed and watched his mouth. All he could do now was breathe. I counted the seconds between each breath. Not with finger taps or eye blinks but with my mind. In those long moments, I finally came to see him as the imperfect man that he was and not the perfect one I had wanted him to be.

I stroked his soft hair and held his hand. We had come full circle. I was his little boy again, and he was sick. Although, this time, I was by his side because I wanted to be, not out of obligation. After my parents split up, the love I felt for my father became heavy and stiff. No matter how hard I threw my love at him, it never once came back. But now it felt light. And so when I whispered in his ear the three words I never thought I would say to him, I carved *I forgive you* into my heart. And now, whenever I throw it out, it comes back again and again, as sure as the setting sun.

Genesis

Whenever the sun went down and night came, Coyote would feel sad, because he could no longer see his friends. Unlike his friends, Coyote didn't sleep. In order to make the night more like the day, Coyote decided to make a candle like the kind humans used.

First, Coyote snuck into houses and stole the bits of candles left over after people had gone to sleep. He took all these leftover candles and started molding them between his hot paws. Coyote did this until he had made a candle as tall as he was. When night came, Coyote lit the candle and was able to see his friends Possum, Skunk, and Raccoon again. When the next night came, there was nothing left of his candle to burn, and so Coyote couldn't find his friends.

Determined to build a bigger candle, Coyote went into all the houses and gathered as much wax as he could. Coyote built his new candle around a tall piece of bamboo that would be the wick he would light when it was done.

Week after week, Coyote's candle grew and grew. When it was the size of a tree, Crow asked him if his candle was big enough. Coyote answered that a candle the size of a tree would not last very long. When there were no more bits of candle to add, Coyote told each of his friends sad stories and collected their dried tears to make his candle bigger.

When Coyote found Possum, he told him the story of how Skunk had been all black once, but one night when he was a baby, he saw a fearsome monster wearing a black mask. The monster scared him so badly he became sick with a fever that lasted five days. At the end of the fever, his hair had turned bright-white down the middle of his back. This story made Possum cry so much that he grew tired and fell asleep. While he was sleeping, Coyote collected all of Possum's tears.

When Coyote found Raccoon, he told her the story about how Possum had been born with a tail as bushy as Raccoon's but how when Possum was a baby, he had heard Skunk screaming after seeing a scary monster wearing a black mask. The screaming had scared Possum so much he had gotten sick with a fever that lasted five days. At the end of the fever, all the hair on his tail had fallen off. This story made Raccoon cry so much that she grew tired and fell asleep. While she was sleeping, Coyote collected all of Raccoon's tears.

When Coyote found Skunk, he told him the story about how Raccoon had not always had black eyes. Because Raccoon was afraid of the dark when she was a baby, she put ashes on her face so that she would have a scary mask to scare away monsters. When the daylight came and Raccoon tried to wash off the mask in the river, it wouldn't come off. This story made Skunk cry so much that he grew tired and fell asleep. While he was sleeping, Coyote collected all of Skunk's tears.

Because Coyote's friends had cried so much, his candle grew and grew until it was the size of a barn. When Coyote went to light his candle, Crow flapped his wings and blew out Coyote's match, because he was afraid Coyote's candle would light the world on fire.

Before Coyote could light another match, Crow grabbed the candle and flew it into the sky where Coyote couldn't reach it. Coyote was so sad he became sick with a fever that lasted five days. On the sixth day, the night came, and the stars heated the tears of his friends and made his candle glow in the night sky. Seeing the moon made Coyote feel better. Coyote and his friends never lost each other in the darkness again.

Acknowledgments

Thank you to the communities at Texas State University, Drew University, and Vermont College of Fine Arts for their support over the years as I worked on this book. A very special thanks to Rice University, the Office of Research, and the School of Humanities for their support of this book and its vision with a Creative Ventures grant.

Heartfelt thanks to my editor Courtney Ochsner for believing in this book and giving me a chance to say something in paragraphs. This book couldn't have found a better home than with you and the fabulous team at University of Nebraska Press.

Of all the resources I consulted on obsessive-compulsive disorder, I owe a special debt to ocdhistory.net for helping broaden my understanding of the historical scope of the disorder.

I could not have written this book without the support of friends. Thank you, James Arthur, for that long walk in Baltimore when you listened to my stories about Jackie and for saying they might be the seeds of a book. Thank you, Erin Evans, for helping me rediscover the music of the typewriter. I doubt I would've been able to compose the first draft without the click-clack-ding of that music. Thank you, Breana Dumbrell, for so generously trading stories and pages about our fathers and their struggles. Thank you, Micah Larson, for giving me the exact book I needed to read when I felt like scrapping the whole thing. Thank you, Jess Smith, for tirelessly reading draft upon draft and for always being a sounding board. Marie Mockett, Sunil Yapa, and Jamie Figueroa, thanks for reading pages and helping me find the shape of this book. Thank you, Patrick Madden, Sue William Silverman, and Harrison Candelaría Fletcher, for helping me find my way in this world of prose.

Hugs and love to my family, Rebecca and the kids and the Booms, Juan and Pam and the kids, my hermanos and hermanas, and all the primos and primas and tíos and tías. And para mi mamá, it's impossible to count all the ways in which you've supported and loved me in this life. I wouldn't be the person I am without you.

To order or obtain more information on these or other University
of Nebraska Press titles, visit nebraskapress.unl.edu.

CPSIA information can be obtained
at www.ICGtesting.com
Printed in the USA
LVHW090523300122
709553LV00004B/426